what people are saying about *God Chicks*...

I have been going through the book with some wo BIG HIT! They have totally grabbed the concept

I just wanted to let you know how much I loved your book: it has totally inspired me. You wrote some things I needed to hear.

—TYLER, TX

Thank you so much for writing this book! I have shared it with so many people. It is the perfect picture of just who woman is!

—CHICAGO, IL

I loved the book so much! I am getting another copy to give to someone who is in the hospital. I know it will be a huge encouragement to her. Thank you!

—PORTLAND, OR

I read *God Chicks* a few weeks ago and it has totally changed my life. When I read about being a "princess chick" I just cried. I had never really understood what it meant to be a daughter of the King. And the chapter on "friend chick" made me grateful for my friends and made me want to be a better one. I have given the book to someone who doesn't have a relationship with God, and I believe the book could lead her there. Thanks for writing such a fantastic book!

—ALBERTA, CANADA

Holly, you are so inspirational! Thank you for your wisdom, humor and passion for life!

—SYDNEY, AUSTRALIA

You are so funny! I have never had anyone get through the walls between my heart and mind so easily. Your free spirit, love for God, and your...oh, how can I say it?...hilarity!...just make that 6 inch drop so easy!

—NASHVILLE, TN

I read your book in two days...I could not put it down! With each page I smiled and learned, and after closing your book I took a new look on life. Three days later I read your book again!!! It didn't just inspire me, but it helped to guide me on a journey I have always known was there...my journey in God's hands. Thank you.

—VALENCIA, CA

It has been on my heart to be a virtuous woman of God. I am 18 years old and I have a heart to shake the nation and change my generation. Thanks for painting the picture of how I can do it!

—LEE'S SUMMIT, MO

Thank you! Thank you for sharing your heart, passion, vision, life-giving words and humor!

—OXFORD, ENGLAND

As I read your book, I was encouraged by your openness…you just being you! I love your sense of humor!

—DALLAS, TX

You left me with many pearls of wisdom. I get married in less than a week and I need all the wisdom I can get!

—SHEFFIELD, ENGLAND

Thank you for bringing inspiration to my life!

—MANCHESTER, ENGLAND

I have just finished your book *God Chicks* …..WOW!!! I loved it! More please!!

—DERBYSHIRE, ENGLAND

Thank you! I just really want you to know what an impact you have had on me. I have been very skeptical of organized religion, because until I heard what you had to say, I have always encountered hypocrites. I have really been waiting for that breath of fresh air that didn't judge, and had only love to offer.

—Auckland, NEW ZEALAND

Thank you for the book. I LOVED IT!! My past has not been a great one, but now I feel that I can finally move forward unhindered.

—CHICAGO, IL

Thank you for being such a great "party chick"!…and for your message on loving each other.

—QUEENSTOWN, NEW ZEALAND

This message has made such an incredible impact on my life and the lives of my daughter, sister, cousin and mother. I am forever grateful!

—LOS ANGELES, CA

I am inspired by your dream for womanhood and commit to run even harder to take this cause to the planet!

—VANCOUVER, CANADA

What a great book! It is the kind of book that every guy should read. It would help men see where a woman should be going in life as a woman of God and in life in general. It is well written, clear – simple, but profound. There was not one weak chapter. This is just an awesome, awesome book.

—PASTOR MIKE CONNAWAY, SEATTLE, WA

WHEN IT POURS HE REIGNS

OVERCOMING LIFE'S STORMS

HOLLY WAGNER

OLIVER NELSON

™

THOMAS NELSON PUBLISHERS®
Nashville

A Division of Thomas Nelson, Inc.
www.ThomasNelson.com

Published in Nashville, Tennessee, by Thomas Nelson, Inc.

Unless otherwise noted, Scripture quotations are from THE AMPLIFIED BIBLE: Old Testament. Copyright © 1962, 1964 by Zondervan Publishing House (used by permission); and from THE AMPLIFIED NEW TESTAMENT. Copyright © 1958 by the Lockman Foundation (used by permission).

Scripture quotations noted CEV are from THE CONTEMPORARY ENGLISH VERSION. © 1991 by the American Bible Society. Used by permission.

Scripture quotations noted NIV are from the HOLY BIBLE: NEW INTERNATIONAL VERSION®. Copyright © 1973, 1978, 1984 by International Bible Society. Used by permission of Zondervan Publishing House. All rights reserved.

Scripture quotations noted THE MESSAGE are taken from *The Message.* Copyright © by Eugene H. Peterson 1993, 1994, 1995. Used by permission of NavPress Publishing Group.

Scripture quotations noted NASB are from the NEW AMERICAN STANDARD BIBLE®. Copyright © The Lockman Foundation 1960, 1962, 1963, 1968, 1971, 1972, 1973, 1975, 1977, 1995. Used by permission.

Scripture quotations noted NCV are from *The Everyday Bible, New Century Version,* copyright © 1987 by Worthy Publishing, Fort Worth, TX 76137. Used by permission.

Scripture quotations noted NLT are from the *Holy Bible,* New Living Translation, copyright © 1996. Used by permission of Tyndale House Publishers, Inc., Wheaton, Illinois 60189. All rights reserved.

Library of Congress Cataloging-in-Publication Data

Wagner, Holly.
    When it pours, He reigns : overcoming life's storms / Holly Wagner.
      p. cm.
    Includes bibliographical references.
    ISBN 0-7852-6449-3 (pbk.)
    1. Christian women—Religious life. I. Title.
BV4527.W3 2004
248.8'6—dc22   2003023970

Printed in the United States of America

04 05 06 07 PHX 8 7 6 5 4 3

To Noriko,
who is riding out one of life's roughest
storms. My friend—you are doing it
with such grace and such a confident
assurance that you are in His hand. In
the midst of the waves, there has not
been a day that I haven't heard you
laugh. You truly are a hero.

contents

contents

a few thoughts from the middle of the storm

most of you probably don't remember where you were at 4:30 A.M. on January 17, 1994—other than in bed! I will never forget. I was fast asleep in bed with my husband, Philip (good place to be!), when suddenly I was violently shaken.

I quickly realized that we were having a very large earthquake here in California. The shaking was terrible, and the noise was even worse. I have since learned that when the earth moves like that, it creates some kind of a sonic boom. All I knew was that it felt like a bomb went off under our home. Our alarm system started going off on top of all of that noise. I could hear all the wedding china—which I had spent hours picking out—hitting the tile floor and shattering into a million pieces.

While the shaking was still going on, Philip yelled that he would go get Paris (our two-and-a-half-year-old daughter) and that I should get our son, Jordan (age six). The house was pitch black. The electricity in the whole city was out, so I didn't even have ambient city light to guide me. I couldn't see my hand in front of my face. As I was stumbling across our bedroom to get to the hall, a dresser flew across the room and clipped me in the legs. Now I was crawling to get to my son.

When I got to his door, I couldn't open it because something had fallen on the other side and blocked it. Being the woman of faith I am, I panicked! I yelled, "Jordan . . . Jordan . . . *Open this door!*" He said, "Mom, I'm all right!" Eventually we got his door open and we stood in the doorway, as you are supposed to do in an earthquake.

Philip was holding Paris in her doorway, and we all held on as the first aftershock hit. This was just a little less intense than the initial jolt, but still frightening. We realized that we needed to get out of the house, so we grabbed a blanket (it was winter, which in Los Angeles can be tough . . . sixty degrees or so!) and made our way downstairs and out to the front lawn. Somebody remembered to get the dog, and we all huddled under the blanket. The most important people in the world to me were under that blanket.

A few houses around us exploded as their gas lines burst.

Burning embers were flying over our heads. Finally the sun began to make its way over the horizon, and we could see the devastation around us. Blood was pouring down my leg where the dresser had hit me. I carry the scars still. In the shock of the moment, I hadn't noticed the injury until that point.

I opened our front door to look inside our house and was stunned at the chaos. Every wall was cracked, the chandelier had swung so hard it had broken a wall, the television and computer had been thrown across the room, all the plates and glasses were shattered, and the kitchen appliances were no longer in the kitchen. In the light of day, it was shocking. This definitely hadn't been on the schedule for my life. The damage came to around seventy thousand dollars. I certainly had uses for that money other than fixing walls! At that moment, I wasn't sure how we would make it.

You may never face an earthquake like that. I certainly hope not! But I am sure that you will face your own challenges that must be handled and overcome. You will face your own midnight. The decisions we make at the stormy, midnight times in our lives are crucial: they determine whether or not we'll make it through. In the midst of that earthquake, Philip and I made some good decisions that led our family to safety, and we almost made some that I believe would have cost us our destiny.

Most of us lead full, busy, expansive lives. We have dreams to dream, goals to reach, and destinies to fulfill. Like me, you have probably realized that life—with its dreams, goals, and destinies—

can be difficult, to say the least!! Sometimes it is downright painful, full of challenges and storms that seem determined to knock us off course. And sometimes, life can seem so dark that any light at the end of the tunnel seems to be only an oncoming train!

When you encounter a storm, don't take it personally. Some storms might be of our making—our own bad choices— but plenty occur simply because we are alive on planet Earth. Storms come to the good and the bad, to the just and the unjust . . . they come to us all. And storms are not optional; they are part of the curriculum of life. They are not "electives," nor are they necessarily punishment for something we or someone else has done wrong. They are essential elements for our growth.

In fact, we are not just to *go* through them, but to *grow* through them.[1]" We face storms in our world, our country, our cities, our families, and within our own hearts. Jesus promised us that in this world we would have trials, distress, and frustration . . . but that we should be at peace, because He has overcome the world for us and shown us how to be victorious!

I was helping one of my children with their homework and learned something interesting. In 1991, eight scientists created an artificial environment in Oracle, Arizona, called Biosphere 2 and lived inside it for two years. (How they managed without a mall and a Starbucks is beyond me!) Inside their self-sustaining community, the scientists created a number of mini-ecosystems, including a desert, a rain forest, and even an ocean. They simulated nearly every weather element except wind. After a while, the effects of their windless environment became apparent. A number of trees bent over and even snapped. Without the stress of wind to strengthen the wood, the trunks grew weak and could not hold their own weight. Like it or not, we have to admit that weathering storms builds our strength.

That strength has a purpose. In my book *God Chicks,* I challenged women to understand and embrace the incredible roles God made us to fulfill. One chapter I called "the warrior chick." You and I are to be warriors on the earth. I am not talking about carrying guns and knives . . . I'm talking about being a force for good on the planet. Proverbs 31:15 challenges us, as God's girls, to rise "while it is yet night." Personally, I used to hate that verse because I thought it meant I had to get up before the sun rose . . . and that sounded horrible to me! The truth is, however, that verse has very little to do with the time of day that we get up and everything to do with being women who rise in the midst of dark times. When everything around us is in the midst of chaos, the warrior chick rises. She does not wilt. She actually grows stronger in the midst of storms.

There were a number of times in the Bible when God raised up a woman to bring strength to others in the darkness. When the children of Israel were in bondage to a foreign king, God heard their cry and used Deborah to lead them to freedom. She was just a girl, like you and me, given an opportunity to rise in the midst of a storm. She accepted the challenge and encouraged military leaders to victory.

Esther was another woman who rose up in the midst of a storm. Even though she was the queen, she was not allowed to see her husband, the king, unless he called for her. However, when she learned that her people were going to be killed, she bravely entered the court of the king and risked her very life to ask for his protection. Because of her courage, a nation of people was saved. It is our obligation as daughters of the King to rise in the storms and not let them sink us. The world is watching to see God in us.

We live in amazing times! It is truly an awesome time to be alive. As I write this, my country is at war, and chaos is evident all over the planet. I think I was born for such a time as this. I was born to help bring the love of God to my generation . . . so were you! But storms get in our way. In my twenty years of ministering to people, I have seen people make amazingly stupid (is that too strong a word?) choices while in the midst of midnight storms. I've made some too! We can all make decisions in our dark times that can jeopardize our very dreams and goals.

I have a very dear friend who, at one point in her life, was emotionally hurting. Her parents' marriage was going through its own storm; some men in her life had let her down; her career wasn't going the way she thought it should . . . storm. So, she decided to do something about the pain she was facing. She went shopping! Now, normally I am all for shopping—but not at the expense of my future. This girl spent thousands in her quest to make herself feel better. It didn't work. Now, a few years later, she has massive debt and has created another storm she must weather.

All throughout life we need to make decisions that produce the future we want. It is the same when we are in a storm. We must choose actions that will get us to shore in one piece! We don't want to make choices that merely create another storm.

When we (scholar, historian, or average person) evaluate our presidents, we choose the best based on the magnitude of the crisis during which he led: George Washington for his leadership during the American Revolution . . . Abraham Lincoln for his guidance during a time when our country was torn in two . . . Franklin D. Roosevelt for his authority during the Depression and the attack on Pearl Harbor. When we go through difficulties, we think life is terrible; but it was the difficulties these men faced that led to their greatness. There is greatness within you, and it becomes apparent as you go through your storm.

In the following pages, I am going to offer some practical ways not only to survive the storms of life (sort of a storm-survival handbook!) but also to come out as winners. Jesus walked in and spoke to storms, and He never allowed them to interfere with His destiny. I believe that demonstrating a victorious way of living, even in challenging times, is our responsibility as children of God.

I will use as a guide the story of the apostle Paul, who was a prisoner on a ship headed for Rome. While traveling, the ship encountered severe storms. For days, the survival of the ship's passengers was questionable. Paul's journey to Rome was not an easy one. Acts 27 records his adventure, and it offers encouragement to those of us who find ourselves at midnight in the midst of a storm. Just like Paul, you and I are living in trying times. Paul did some very specific things to survive his storm, and these are the same things we must also do to make it through ourselves.

I am writing this book because I want to see each woman fulfill her purpose. It will not be handed to us on silver platters. Darn! And remember, we never camp out in the storm . . . we get through it. Just like you have to go through Denver if you want to get from one coast to the other (and you are flying United). I'm not staying in Denver (not that Denver isn't lovely!), just passing through. We don't stay in the valley of the shadow of death . . . we follow our Shepherd through it.

The Bible offers guidance for those of us who find ourselves at midnight in the midst of a storm. Get ready to push through it. Paul said that we are one body . . . each dependent on the other. I am counting on you to get through your storms. Please don't quit. Heaven—and humanity—are counting on us.

...two are better than one... Old Testament, Ecclesiastes Chapter 4, Verse 9a

COURAGE IS ACTING
WITH FEAR, NOT
WITHOUT IT.
—WALTER ANDERSON

one

PUT YOUR BRACES ON!

*The sailors wrapped ropes
around the ship to hold it
together. They used supports
with ropes to undergird and
brace the ship.*

—New Testament, Acts 27,
verse 17 (CEV, amplified)

I was crossing a small part of the athletic field at my elementary school by hanging on to a rope stretched twelve feet above the ground. I wasn't trying to be Indiana Jones, I was merely a part of a PE class. Hand over hand, I made my way, dangling above the ground. I was doing just fine when suddenly my hands slipped, and I fell to the ground. *Snap!* There went the bone in my wrist. I was in pain, but I was more embarrassed that I hadn't made it across the field like the boys did . . . most of the other girls didn't even try. I was still at the age where I was trying to prove that anything a boy could do . . . so could I! A teacher rushed me to the doctor's office, where I got a cast put on my arm.

I am sure that many of you have broken a bone at one time or another, or maybe your children have. So you are familiar with the fact that the cast holds the reset bone in place so that it can heal correctly. The cast acts as a brace, a support mechanism, so that the bone can regain its strength. Without the cast, the patient would suffer a lot of pain and have no guarantee that the bone would heal straight.

When Paul's ship was encountering an incredibly severe storm, the crew put ropes under the vessel to hold it together. Can you imagine how frightening it must have been for the sailor who had to take the rope, jump into the stormy sea, swim under the ship, come up on the other side with the rope, tie it down—and then do it again? Whew! And I think running two miles on the treadmill is work! The sailors knew, though, that if they were going to make it through the storm, they had to brace the ship so that it wouldn't break apart in the rough seas they were in. It is the same for you and me. If we are going to survive the storms of life, one of the things we must do is put our braces on.

In the middle of a storm you might be facing, whether it is in your marriage (and if you have been married longer than six minutes, you have encountered some storms!), your health, your career, or your finances, you need to put some support mechanisms in place in order to make it to shore . . . which is always the goal!

GET YOUR THINKING STRAIGHT

In those weeks after the earthquake of 1994, we experienced thousands of aftershocks. Basically, that means that our earth was never still. I hated it! Every time the ground shook, so did I. I wondered if another quake was coming that would finally cause southern California to float off into the Pacific Ocean. The jokes about Arizona becoming beachfront property weren't so funny anymore! I truly was afraid, and I realized that I needed to fight the fear if I was going to make it.

The apostle Peter challenged us to brace up our minds . . . to think straight. When going through any storm, we must take control of our thoughts. This is the first support mechanism: getting our thinking straight.

So, to deal with the fear I was feeling, I opened my Bible. The book of Psalms is a great place to start. King David, who wrote most of the book, had to deal with fear regularly. He had a number of enemies who wanted him dead, so he had some things to say about it! In Psalm 118, I read that when I turn to God, He will take my worries away. When He is on my side, I don't need to fear. In Psalm 91 David wrote that when I make Him my refuge, His angels protect me . . . (and I don't need to worry about the dangers at night). I said that particular part aloud, because there were nights I was worried. Every slight earth tremor sent me sitting up in bed. To deal with this fear, I quoted those passages *out loud*, so that my mind could hear them! To survive this

MAY I SUGGEST, HOWEVER, THAT THE FACTS ARE NOT NEARLY AS IMPORTANT AS THE TRUTH. TO MAKE IT THROUGH THE STORMS, OUR LIVES MUST BE BUILT ON TRUTH . . . NOT JUST FACTS.

storm of fear, I had to brace up my mind. I had to control my thoughts.

I love learning different facts about all sorts of things. My husband says I have too many trivial facts in my brain (trivial being his word!). That is because I am always reading something. Hey, it also makes me good at game shows! (After I won thousands of dollars on a game show one time, he began to appreciate the stuff I store in my brain!) It is always better if we base our opinions of different circumstances on actual facts. I actually get frustrated with people who spout off opinions without a factual basis. May I suggest, however, that the facts are not nearly as important as the truth. To make it through the storms, our lives must be built on truth . . . not just facts.

Declare the Truth!

We are changed, transformed, when our minds are renewed, not necessarily when the circumstances change. As a young woman in her early twenties, my friend Sarah was diagnosed with Hodgkin's disease and had to undergo chemotherapy . . . not just one round of treatment, but two. A great example of bracing one's mind came after one of her chemotherapy treatments. She was sick, as many people get after chemotherapy, and was throwing up.

Now, I don't know about you, but I hate throwing up. I am not a delicate throw-upper. And I always feel sorry for myself as I am hanging over the toilet. But not Sarah. Her husband said that in between bouts of nausea, she would declare what the Bible said about her—not necessarily the facts of her situation. Here's the scenario: *throw up* . . . *"I am a daughter of the King"* *(Psalm 45)* . . . *throw up* . . . *"He was wounded so that I might be healed" (see 1 Peter 2:24)* . . . *throw up* . . . *"I am an overcomer"* . . . *throw up* . . . *"I will make it through this!"* Sarah was putting her braces on. She had to, if she was going to make it through that storm.

Some of you are experiencing a storm in your health; or maybe someone you love is in the middle of one. I truly am sorry. Try what Sarah did. Declare the truth in the midst of the circumstance; don't let the facts of the doctor's report defeat you.

> WHERE YOU BEGAN WILL SEEM UNIMPORTANT BECAUSE YOUR FUTURE WILL BE SO SUCCESSFUL.
> —OLD TESTAMENT, JOB 8, VERSE 7 (NCV)

Another friend, Christine, recently uncovered some facts about her life. At the age of thirty-two, she found out that the people she had always called Mom and Dad were not, in fact, her biological parents. She was shocked, to say the least. After she found out that she had been adopted, she asked for and received a number of government papers in the mail. She read the social worker's report from thirty-three years ago, which said that the baby (Christine) was unwanted, and the woman who gave birth to her just wanted it all to be over with so that she could get on with her life. When Christine was born, she lay in a crib without a name or a parent.

Finding out that you were unwanted and unnamed at birth could certainly throw you. This is a real storm. And it could be scary. But honestly, it didn't knock Christine off course. Why? Because the facts concerning her birth didn't change the truth of her life. She declared the truth over her life, which is . . . *Before God formed her in the womb (whoever's womb that was!), He knew her (Jer. 1:5). He created her wonderfully (Ps. 139:14). He destined her to have a future filled with hope (Jer. 29:11).* The facts of her birth: unnamed and unwanted. The truth: formed by God, wonderfully created, and a loved-beyond-measure daughter of the King. Because Christine hung on to the truth, she is walking confidently in the knowledge of who she is. Today she travels all over the globe, motivating and inspiring thousands of people to love the God who loves them.

Maybe some of you reading this can relate to the shock of finding out that the circumstances of your birth weren't what you thought. Brace yourself with the truth. Don't let the facts mess you up!

a Marital Storm

There was a time (okay, actually more than one!) when my marriage was definitely in a midnight storm. Of course, it was all *Philip's* fault! If only he could be more like me. After all, I was practically perfect! The first few years of our marriage were especially trying . . . because I was just realizing that Cinderella lied.

Philip was neither a prince nor charming, and I was ready

THE FIRST FEW YEARS OF OUR MARRIAGE WERE ESPECIALLY TRYING . . . BECAUSE I WAS JUST REALIZING THAT CINDERELLA LIED.

to throw the slipper at him. (I'm sure he felt similarly!) There were just too many differences between us, and I wasn't sure we could make it. The scary thing is, I had begun to lose hope. In fact, I was starting to pack my bags when suddenly I plopped myself to the floor and began to declare the truth.

The facts were overwhelming . . . too many differences (personalities, backgrounds, and families); he had had no role model for how to be a husband; I was very stubborn; he could be moody and unaffectionate; we weren't happy . . . and the list goes on. I had to say the truth out loud: "Marriage is 'precious, of great price, and especially dear' (Heb. 13:4). My husband is deeply in love with me . . . he is rejoicing with me, the wife of his youth (Prov. 5:18). If I ask God for the wisdom and understanding necessary to build our home, I will get it (James 1:5). 'Love never fails' (1 Cor. 13:8)."

I hope I am not making it sound easy, because it wasn't. My marriage was at a crisis point. I am sure that some of you understand. I almost gave up. The facts were too freaky.

But now, eighteen years later, I am more in love with my husband than ever, and we have a great life—not without its challenges, but great, nonetheless—with two awesome children, a flourishing church, and wonderful friends around the planet. I shudder to think of what I almost gave up because the facts were too overwhelming in that dark moment. Our marriage didn't get better overnight, but from the moment I started declaring the truth, there were small signs of improvement. I read books on how to build a marriage, Philip and I went to seminars, and we quit blaming each other for the storm.

Maybe your marriage is in the center of a storm. You might have given up on a marriage in the past. I am not here to criticize or to judge. Regardless of whether you are working on marriage number one or marriage number twelve, make this the one you finish out life with. Don't let the storms in the marriage sink you. If the facts are scary, declare the truth!

As the young shepherd David faced the Philistines, he heard the facts about his enemy, Goliath. Fact: Goliath was a giant . . . would have made Shaquille O'Neal look puny. David was a youth. Fact: Goliath had top-notch weapons. David had a used slingshot. Fact: Goliath had years of military experience. David had never seen a battle before. But all those facts paled next to the truth: David was loved and anointed by God for victory. So are you.

The Part Friends Play

Recently, my friend Joyce went through a severe financial storm. She had been very successful for many years as a television producer. Suddenly, the work dried up, and she encountered some unexpected expenses. She began having more month than money. I am sure some of you can relate! The facts did not look good. So she began declaring the truth. *Because she is a tither, God would open windows of heaven and pour out a blessing . . . so big, she can't contain it (Mal. 3:10). He would supply all that she needed according to His riches (Phil. 4:19).*

Of course, she didn't just stay home and quote Scripture. She went out looking for work and continued to give of what she had. A tip for free: We all reap what we sow. If we want finances, we have to give them. If we want love, we have to give it. Joyce could rest, knowing that God would meet the needs she had.

However Joyce had to learn to do something else in this particular storm. She had always been very proud of the fact that, as a single mother, she had raised two smart and healthy kids without having to lean on anyone else financially. It was wonderful that she had been so successful all by herself . . . but in this storm, she was going to have to learn to ask for help.

For Joyce, this was very hard. She had to let go of her pride and humble herself. She finally did, and because Joyce had been such a big giver to the person she asked, he was glad to share with Joyce. She got the help she needed and learned the value of relationships.

Okay, so we put our braces on by putting support mechanisms in place. The first support mechanism is declaring the truth. The second support mechanism is—each other!

You + Friend = Survival in Storms

Author Stu Weber illustrated the need to have a buddy:

The war in Vietnam was building to its peak, and one stop for young army officers was the U.S. Army Ranger School at Fort Benning. The venerable, steely-eyed veteran told the soldiers that the next nine weeks would test their mettle as it had never been tested.

The sergeant said many wouldn't make the grade—it was just too tough. (Turned out he was right. Of 287 in the formation that day, only 110 finished the nine weeks.)

I can still hear that raspy voice cutting through the morning humidity like a serrated blade. "We are here to save your lives," he preached. "We're going to see to it that you overcome all your natural fears—especially of height and water. We're going to show you just how much incredible stress the human mind and body can endure. And when we're finished with you, you will be the U.S. Army's best. You will not only survive in combat, you will accomplish your mission!"

Then, before he dismissed the formation, the hardened Ranger sergeant announced our first assignment. We'd steeled ourselves for something really tough—running 10 miles in full battle gear or rappelling down a sheer cliff. So his first order caught us off guard.

He told us to find a buddy. Some of us would have preferred the cliff. "This is step one," he growled. "You need to find yourself a Ranger buddy. You will stick together. You will never leave each other. You will encourage each other, and, as necessary, you will carry each other."

It was the Army's way of saying, "Difficult assignments require a friend. Together is better. You need someone to help you accomplish the tough course ahead."[1]

God did not create you and me to go through life alone. We are a part of an awesome company of women around the planet. We will fulfill what God created us to do only by getting and staying connected with those who join us on the journey. We were not created to solve all of life's problems on our own. We do not have all of the answers. We need each other!

Some of you have made it through tremendous storms, and other women out there need to know how you did it. Perhaps you single-handedly raised your children into responsible adults (a miracle for any of us!). I guarantee you there are women in your circle of influence who need to know what you did and how you did it. Some of you have overcome tremendous marital storms, managed to stay married for fifty years, and still love that man! We need to know what you know. The same is true for those of you who have lived through tremendous abuse and found the path of healing, and for those of you who have overcome serious debt. Your past can help give someone else a future . . . but only if you are willing to build relationships. There is also someone out there who can help give you hope in the storm you are going through—if you reach out.

King Solomon said it best: "Two are better than one . . . If one falls down [goes through a storm], his friend can help him up."

ISOLATION LEADS TO POWERLESSNESS

Sometimes in the animal kingdom, if one animal is suffering, it will go off by itself. However a proverb tells us that she who isolates herself rages against all wisdom. We can't go off by ourselves to lick our wound . . . No! We have to give and get support from each other.

I remember an older woman who had been coming to our church for a while, always remaining on the outskirts of the congregation. One day she came to me and described a crisis she was in. I felt horrible for her and offered what help I could. What made me sad was that she had no real friends with whom she was close. She did not have one friend to stand with her in this situation. I tried to connect her to others so that she could get through the storm in one piece! Life can be tough. (You've probably figured that out by now!) Thank God for friends to help us get through.

I read recently about a woman who was driving from Alberta, Canada, to the Yukon. She didn't know that no one should ever travel that way alone—especially in a rundown car—because she'd have to cross an especially rugged mountain pass, and the weather was foggy. So she set off on a road usually reserved for four-wheel-drive trucks.

Eventually, she found herself in a truck stop. Two truckers invited her to join them, and since the place was small, she felt obligated to oblige. "Where are you headed?" one of the truckers asked. She told him and he responded, "In that little car? No way! The pass is dangerous in weather like this."

"Well, I'm determined to try," was her naïve response.

"Then I guess we're going to have to hug you," the trucker said.

"There's no way I'm going to let you touch me," she replied.

The trucker laughed and explained, "Not that. We'll put one truck in front of you and one in the rear. That way, we'll get you through the mountains."

That entire day, she followed the two red brake lights in the fog in front of her, while two headlights hugged her from behind. She did indeed make it over the pass.

That's exactly what the right companions will do for our spiritual journey.[2]

Here's another example. Last winter, I went skiing with my children and a friend of my son. Philip would have gone also, but just the week before he had herniated a disk . . . so he was home flat on his back. We had already paid for the trip, so off I went with the kids! One day I decided to ski with the boys for a run. That was my first mistake! They like the black-diamond runs, and the truth is, I am not a black-diamond skier. I like to enjoy the scenery while calmly making my way down the blue runs to the lodge to get hot chocolate—a perfect ski run to me. But this day I was with the boys.

We got off the lift and quickly took off over a ledge. Next mistake: I didn't look beyond the ledge before I actually skied over it. When I landed on the other side, I quickly realized that I was in serious trouble. This run hadn't gotten a lot of snow, so bushes and trees were peeking through . . . not to mention the fact that it was an almost vertical drop. (Well, it looked like that to my freaked-out eyes!) My son and his friend were about a quarter of the way down when I screamed. I was sure it was going to be my last day on Earth.

Jordan stopped and looked back at his crazy mother. I told him (trying not to cry) that there was no way I was going to make it down the hill. He and his friend climbed back up to me (no easy feat), and we tried to figure out a way to get me to the bottom. Taking my skis off and sliding on my rear end was not an option—the slope was too steep and I would just roll, probably crashing into bushes and trees. That did not sound too fun. Eventually we came up with a plan. Well actually the boys did while I was still fighting panic. Jordan uses snow blades, which are very short, thicker skis. Their shorter length meant he could maneuver around bushes more easily.

We took off my skis, and I held on to a branch, putting my boots on Jordan's shoulders as a brace. His friend held my skis. I am not a lightweight, so my son had to bear my weight as well as the sharp points of my boots as the three of us worked our way down the mountain. It was a slow process . . . me grabbing onto one branch at a time, slowly lowering myself, with Jordan below me, keeping my feet on his sholders. They did it! Those boys got me down. I was so grateful . . . I did a lot of hugging. They endured that, and Jordan calmly patted me, saying, "We'll see you back at the room, Mom." They then took off, as if they hadn't just saved my life!

We do need others to help us get through the tough times.

Everyone Is Lonely in a Storm

From the cross, in the midst of His storm, Jesus asked for a drink. It was a reminder that it's good to have people to help us make it through a storm. A storm can blur our perspective, fog our minds, and tempt our hearts to say things that are not wise, unless we are willing to let our need be known to others. When going through a storm, we'll find that humbling ourselves enough to ask for others' assistance can strengthen our trust in God. Strengthening ourselves—and acknowledging our need of others—is crucial to our survival.

If the Son of God requested help during His struggle, I would be wise to remember that I need to ask for help. This is neither immature nor self-pitying. It is the balance Paul taught the Galatians: "We each must carry our own load"—handle our own responsibilities; "Offer each other a helping hand"—help our friends with their overload.[3]

There will be times, as we go through storms, that we will

feel overloaded and overwhelmed, and can't remember what the truth is anymore. That is when we need each other.

If we are going to make it to shore, we must brace ourselves. We utilize support mechanisms. We declare the truth—we brace our minds. And we brace ourselves by asking for help from a friend.

Just a thought: Wouldn't it be sad, if in your looking around for friends to help, you couldn't see any? So work on relationships and friendships all the time . . . take moments out of your busy life and connect with someone. Don't wait until you are sinking! When you're in a storm and looking for a familiar face . . . you'll find one with whom you have taken the time to build a meaningful relationship.

How beautiful are the feet of those who bring good news! New Testament, Romans, Chapter 10, Verse 15

LIFE IS NOT THE WAY
IT'S SUPPOSED TO BE.
IT'S THE WAY IT IS.
THE WAY YOU DEAL
WITH IT IS WHAT
MAKES THE DIFFERENCE.

—VIRGINIA SATIR

TWO

SEE THE HOPE—
GIVE THE HOPE

*Cheer up! I am sure that
God will do exactly what
he promised.*

—New Testament,
ACTS 27:35 (CEV)

I have gotten in trouble when I have told someone in the midst of a storm to "cheer up." Actually it could be dangerous . . . it's a good way to get smacked! And honestly, I'm not sure *I* want to hear that either—not when I am in struggling through a midnight storm. Paul challenged us to "rejoice with those who rejoice; mourn with those who mourn." So, before we tell someone to cheer up, maybe we should share her grief. We should be great at listening and understanding someone's pain. (I'm sorry if you are in the midst of a storm right now, and no one is comforting or listening to you. I pray that someone comes along who can sympathize and give you a hug.)

A time will come, however, when hope must again rule your heart . . . if you ever want to get out of the storm. Only we can control our own attitudes. Our circumstances do not determine our attitude; neither do other people. We read many times in the Psalms that when David was at a low point, he basically told his soul (his mind, will, and emotions) rejoice. We do have authority over our emotions. And right now, if you feel as if your emotions are running away with you—get them back!

As I mentioned in the introduction, Jesus promised us that in this world we would have tribulations and tough times (thank You very much!), but in the very next breath, He said that we should be of good cheer because He has overcome the world. Yes, you will encounter storms, but be of good cheer . . . lighten up! He will see you through!

I have heard that man can live about forty days without food, three days without water, eight minutes without air . . . but only one second without hope. When hopelessness fills your heart, death begins to take over—death to your dreams. The power of hope coursing through your veins can be your most valuable asset, because it creates a tremendous force in your life. Hope is not a luxury; it is an essential. Hope can change tragedy to opportunity, dreaded work to exciting worthwhile effort, weariness to invincibility. If we are going to make it to shore, we must build hope again in our hearts.

> I have heard that man can live about forty days without food, three days without water, eight minutes without air . . . but only one second without hope.

FOLLOW THE LEADER

One of my favorite Bible verses says, "In Christ, God leads us from place to place in one perpetual victory parade." I am certainly not a Bible scholar, but I have learned a few things about that verse. Paul was referring to the victory parade Caesar gave when one of his Roman generals succeeded in a military campaign. In this parade there was dancing, music, and cheering (and, I am sure, confetti!). The conquering general rode in a great chariot pulled by white horses, and his army followed. They all shared in the glory of the celebration Caesar threw on behalf of the military leader. What an awesome sight it must have been! The picture for you and me is this: Jesus is our conquering General. You and I are part of His army—the warrior chicks!—and share in the victory. He leads us in one perpetual victory parade.

The message of Christianity is victory! We need to see ourselves riding in the parade. We are not trudging through a world of misery. Because of what Jesus did, we are in nothing less than a victory celebration! We'd better practice our parade wave, and get the smile ready. I believe this Scripture says not that we are fighting for victory . . . but that we are fighting from a place of victory. We are truly "more than conquerors"! I love this picture!

Wouldn't it be great if life were one mountaintop experience after another? It is easy to believe God is on our side when so much good stuff is going on in our lives. It is easy to have hope when we are on the mountaintop. But the truth is, every mountain has a valley. We will face storms between here and the shore. Yet we are still in the victory parade! While Jesus told us that we would encounter trials, distress, and frustration, He also said He has "deprived the world of power to harm" and knock us off course.

Jesus paid a great price for us to walk in this parade—to fulfill our destinies. Let's do it! God's intention, no matter what valley or storm we face, is for us to overcome. He is the God of valleys and storms. Never lose sight of that! Let that be the foundation of your hope.

As someone like you who is doing her best to ride out the storms of life, let me say this: We have a responsibility as His daughters. We actually don't have the luxury of camping out in the valleys or letting the storms sink us. We are supposed to be examples to those out there who may not know Him; we are to show them how to live a victorious life—not a perfect one—just committed to the parade, regardless of circumstances. Isaiah challenges me every time I read what he wrote. He said that we are to *arise* from the depression in which circumstances have kept us—rise to a new life. In fact, we are supposed to shine! He said that darkness is covering the earth (boy, isn't that the truth?), but that the glory of God will be visible in you and me so that people who are hurting can come to us for answers.

Keep the Share in Sight

To build hope within, you must keep your focus on where you are going. (I will talk more about this in Chapter 5.) We will encounter all different kinds of storms. I have recently been in a fairly small storm . . . but a storm, nonetheless.

Because of some hereditary issues, and an accident or two, I have spent countless hours in dentists' and oral-surgeons' chairs. Recently I had to undergo some more dental work. Sigh. I put on my brave face and spent about seven hours in one sitting, with my mouth open and that little suction thingy (so technical, I know!) making lots of noise. Oh, and let's not forget the sound of the high-pitched drill running for hours straight . . . the metal crown remover thumping in my head . . . and needles being stuck in the roof of my mouth. Are you feeling sorry for me yet?

Throughout this ordeal, I kept my hope, because I kept before me the picture of how beautiful my teeth were going to look. I kept thinking about how much better they would be when the dentist was finished with me. In this long process, I went back for a few visits, and by the time we were done, I had spent about twenty-five hours in the chair. Yuck! And just when I thought we were done, I found out she had made a mistake. So, I had to go back to the chair with the suction thingy, the metal pounder, and the needle in the roof of my mouth . . . and we went through the whole process again. Once again, I got through it because of the hope set before me of having great teeth.

Needless to say, I don't care if I ever see this dentist again! Now, I realize this was not a life-threatening storm (well actually, there were times when I wanted to threaten the dentist's life!), but can I suggest that the principle for getting through all storms, big and small, is the same? We have to keep our hope.

Joy Is a Choice

In the midst of life and in the storms, we must also choose to find joy.

One day, a wealthy father took his son on a trip to the country with the firm purpose of showing the boy how poor people live. The son spent a couple of days and nights on an impoverished family's farm. On the journey home, the father asked, "How was the trip?"

"It was great, Dad."

"Did you see how poor people live?"

"Oh, yeah."

"So, what did you learn?"

The son answered, "I saw that we have one dog, and they had four. We have a pool that reaches to the middle of our garden, and they have a creek that has no end. We have imported lanterns in our garden, and they have the stars at night. Our patio stretches to the front yard, and they have the whole horizon. We have a small piece of land to live on, and they have fields that go beyond our sight. We have servants who serve us, but they serve others. We buy our food, but they grow theirs. We have walls around our property to protect us, they have friends to protect them."

At this, the boy's father was speechless. Then his son added, "Thanks, Dad, for showing me how poor we are."

Too many times we forget what we have and concentrate on what we don't. What is one person's worthless object is another's prize possession. It is all based on one's perspective. Makes you wonder what would happen if we all gave thanks for all the bounty we have instead of worrying about wanting more.[1]

Again, we must *choose* to find joy. I use the word *choose,* because rarely do we *feel* joy when we are in a storm. The apostle James instructed us that if we want to be perfect (and who doesn't?), we will learn to find joy in the midst of difficulties. It is *the* way we will be fully developed and made strong. Most of us can smile when things are going our way, but I suggest that a courageous storm fighter is one who can smile when it seems nothing is going her way. That's power.

How Joy Makes You Strong

Recently a woman in England who had listened to a teaching series of mine on tape approached me. The messages she heard were on finding joy and choosing to live in the parade. She had been going through a really hard time, dealing with hurt, betrayal, and jealousy, and she felt very beaten down. She had lost that happy feeling! Understandable. The first time she listened to the series, she said she just cried (not exactly the response I was going for!). But then she listened to the tapes again and again, until she got it. She—not circumstance—was to control her joy.

This woman hugged me and thanked me. It is always nice when the messages I labor over actually do help someone! Now, a year later, she is a woman more determined than ever not to let situations define her. She still faces challenges (we all will), but she chooses joy in the midst of them. Choosing joy has actually made her stronger. That's how it works.

Author Bunny Wilson is an incredible woman. Recently I heard her speak at a seminar, and as she was walking to the stage, I noticed that her hand was shaking. As soon as she reached the podium, she commented on her shaking hand. She explained that she had gone to see a doctor and had tests run. The conclusion was that she had a generational tremor. Her mother had it, and her older brother had gotten it as he approached the age of fifty. Bunny, now fifty, had a shaking hand. While she is wanting a miracle healing—who wouldn't?— she is smiling in the midst of this storm. She told about a conversation with her ten-year-old daughter.

She and her daughter Gabrielle were trying to figure out what was good about a shaking hand. Gabrielle commented on the fact that Bunny would be a great flag waver at a parade.

Then Gabrielle realized she would be skillful at scratching backs—she could do it without moving her arm! And how about stirring a pot on the stove? She would be perfect at it! I was in awe as I watched my friend look for the good in the midst of her trial. She stands on platforms and speaks to thousands of women. I am sure she is not thrilled with the tremor, but somehow, some way, she is choosing to see the good.

My husband and son recently visited a coin store. The owner told them that most people make the mistake of cleaning all of their old coins before bringing them in to sell. They think that being clean increases the value. They are wrong. Rather than calling the black stuff on old coins "tarnish," we should call it "being toned." Toning actually makes them worth *more*.

Many of us might be feeling a bit tarnished. We think we have lost value. But I would like to suggest that we are merely toned—and thus growing in value. This storm you are in is toning you. It can be your ceiling in life, or a stepping-stone to your future. It is all in how you see it.

I don't know what challenge, trial, or storm you are facing. I don't know where it falls on a scale from one to ten. Maybe you are in the midst of utter devastation. I am sorry. If I were standing next to you, I would hug you and let you cry on my shoulder. Eventually, however, I would encourage you to search for the joy. Joy isn't some flighty, fluffy emotion. It is far more powerful than being "happy." It is the steel that runs through your body. It is your strength.

Throw a Party
(But Leave the Pity at Home)

If you are in a storm, why not have an "I'm Looking for the Joy Party"? Sometimes we withdraw when we go through the tough stuff. I'm suggesting that you throw a party instead. Send out invitations! Say, "I'm going through the worst month of my life (I've gotten a bad doctor's report . . . I lost my job . . . or whatever), and I would like you to come over and help me find my joy. You bring the ice cream." I'm not suggesting that you act as if you are not having a hard time or that you pretend everything is all right. I am just suggesting that if we are to survive the storm without killing anyone(!), we will need to find our joy and keep hope alive. I am suggesting that in spite of the hard time you are going through, you look for something good. And sometimes we need others' help to find it.

Focus on what you do have. Concentrate on the blessings in your life. It is easy to quickly lose sight of anything good while we are under the weight of the storm . . . but try!

I just got off the phone with Helen, a dear friend of mine. She had been at the physical therapist's office because she hurt her neck. They put her in traction for a while . . . I'm not sure why, but I'm sure it helps. Sounds painful to me. Well, while she was stretched out in traction, she decided she could read. So she began to read my book *God Chicks,* which I had just sent her a few days ago. She got to one chapter and a whole bunch of confetti fell out all over her and the floor. (I admit . . . I put it there!)

She said she just laughed. How appropriate . . . a little party in the midst of a storm.

Realize that Jesus has empowered us to get through whatever storm we are fighting. He, the Son of God, told us to "cheer up!" He said He would provide all we need to get through the blustery wind and waves. I'm not sure what you are facing—divorce papers, bankruptcy, a chronic illness—but you are not alone. You can do it!

> WHEN we know HIM as SHEPHERD . . . we remember that our lives are cups overflowing with goodness.

I'm not exactly sure when David wrote the Twenty-third Psalm, but I'm sure it was during one of the many storms he had to overcome in his life. He said that, even though he was walking through a very dark valley (probably couldn't see the next step), he wasn't afraid. Why? Because he knew the Lord as his Shepherd. When we know the Shepherd, then we don't fear, because we know that He will guide us to green pastures and still waters. When we know Him as Shepherd, we don't see our lives as tough times in the valley; we remember that our lives are cups overflowing with goodness.

Hope: See It, Share It

I want to expand the challenge about hope. Not only are we to work hard at keeping it alive in our hearts, but we also are to be people who give it away. I am going to ask you to be a giver, even in the midst of your storm. Take your eyes off of yourself, and find some way that you can contribute to the life of someone else. Find a charity you can give some time to. Offer an encouraging word to a passerby. Give a smile to everyone with whom you come in contact. Listen to someone else's sad story (don't try to top it with yours!). Give blood. One of the dangers of a storm is that we can become very self-focused. We may never get out of the turmoil if we are constantly obsessing over our own lives.

One day Jesus and the boys had been working hard—performing miracles, casting out unclean spirits—just the typical work of Jesus! At the end of the day, they were probably hungry, and since there was no fast-food drive-through, Simon Peter thought of the next best thing. He said, "Why don't we go by my mother-in-law's house? She'll feed us!" So they did. But when they got there, his mother-in-law was sick. I guess they could have made their own sandwiches, but they decided to pray for the mother-in-law instead . . . maybe her sandwiches tasted better (☺). Jesus went to the woman, took her by the hand, and raised her up. The fever left her, and the Bible tells us that she began to wait on Jesus and His disciples.

Now, I don't know about you, but the first time I read this, I thought, *Sheesh! The woman had just had a fever. Couldn't they give her a minute to wipe the sweat off her brow? Better yet, why couldn't they make their own dinner, and let the woman recuperate fully?* (Okay, so my mind can be a bit weird!) But then I realized that the woman showed the right response: she gave. In spite of maybe feeling a bit weak, she served.

Shlomo Breznitz, a psychologist and professor at the University of Haifa in Israel, talks about the importance of giving:

> When we study all of the research from the concentration camps, the first factor that comes up is the ability to establish meaningful relationships in the camps themselves. At first it was thought that it was the recipients who most benefited. Closer examination revealed that it was the givers who were most helped. They were able to maintain dignity and a sense of self . . . The great lesson in this research is that the best way to help oneself is to help someone else.

a Friend to Steer the Ship

When Lynn Eib was diagnosed with colon cancer at the age of thirty-six, her surgeon told her the disease had spread to several lymph nodes. "I had a 40 percent chance of survival," Eib says. "I figured I'd die." Instead, the former journalist struggled through surgery, chemotherapy, and the confusing world of cancer terminology. She worried about what would happen to her three young daughters and husband if she didn't survive.

It was the loneliest time of Eib's life, and when her treatment was complete, she never wanted to step foot inside an oncologist's office again. Yet, deep down she knew other patients were battling the same anxiety and despair she'd faced.

Today, Eib, now forty-nine, helps patients navigate their cancer diagnoses and treatments. "I give them information about their cancer, as well as a list of support groups they can join," she says. "If patients are alone, I'll even take notes for them during a doctor's appointment. I'm there if they need to talk. When I introduce myself as a cancer survivor, I have instant credibility."[2] Eib has found a way to share her hope.

There is an ancient tale told about a widow whose only son has died. She appeals to the holy man of her village to give her a prayer, a potion, *something,* to bring back her boy. He directs her to find and to return to him a mustard seed from a home that has not known sorrow. "The mustard seed is magic," the holy man promises. "I will use it to remove the sorrow from your life."

The first house she comes to is a lavish building occupied by a wealthy family. When the family responds to her knocking, she explains her intentions—that she seeks a mustard seed from a home that has not known sorrow. "You've come to the wrong house," the family members advise the widow, recounting the series of tragedies that had befallen them.

The widow, made sensitive by her own loss, feels great sympathy for the family and decides to stay a while and comfort them. When she leaves, she resumes her search for the magic mustard seed. She visits the high, the low, the middle, the rich, the poor. Everywhere she goes, she finds homes with troubles—and she ministers to all she can help.

She is so busy helping others, in time she forgets her quest for the mustard seed—and she never realizes that it *was* magic: It drove the sorrow from her own life.[3]

The verse I started this chapter with has Paul telling everyone to "cheer up!" Remember, the ship Paul was on was encountering a disastrous storm. He was supposed to be a prisoner on this voyage, but he never saw himself that way. Rather than focusing on whatever injustices he faced, he was the one offering hope and encouragement.

Despite All: Hope

Here is the story of another hope-filled person.

From 1914 to 1916, Ernest Shackleton and his men survived the wreck of their ship, *Endurance,* in the crushing Antarctic ice. They were stranded twelve hundred miles from civilization with no means of communication and no hope for rescue. The temperatures were so low the men could hear the water freeze. They subsisted on a diet of penguins, dogs, and seals. And when the ice began to break up, Shackleton set out to save them all on his heroic eight-hundred-mile trip across the frigid South Atlantic . . . in little more than a rowboat. Unlike most other polar expeditions, every man survived . . . not only in good health, but also in good spirits . . . all due to the leadership of Shackleton.[4]

I hate being cold. The only time I am willing to tolerate it is when I am snow skiing. (I know—I am a wuss!) I also don't like the thought of being in bad weather—much less being *frozen* in it for two years! Ernest Shackleton and his crew were stuck in the Antarctic for just that long, and they not only survived but came out strong. How? One of the reasons is that Ernest remembered to "laugh and joke." He was a "most cheerful person . . . overflowing with optimism and energy." He encouraged his crew to play as well as work together. They performed skits, held sing-alongs, celebrated birthdays, and every Saturday night they gave the traditional seamen's toast to "Sweethearts and Wives."[5]

Ernest wasn't blind to the challenge before them. He just knew that if they were going to survive it, he, as their leader, had not only to have hope but had to give it away. It was more than a feeling; it was a decision. There are times when circumstances can absolutely swamp us. I know—sometimes hope seems very far away. That is when we have to *choose* it. There are people in our lives who are counting on us, and we can't let hopelessness settle in our hearts. Is it easy? No. Can it be done? Yes!

The prophet Isaiah penned some powerful words. He said that God's Spirit rested on Christ (and now on us) for a reason: to share good news with the poor, comfort those whose hearts are broken, tell the captives they are free and the prisoners they are released. We are also to give them a crown to replace their ashes, and the oil of gladness for their sorrow, and the clothes of praise to replace their spirit of sadness. When we do this, the ruins of lives will be rebuilt.

Isaiah also said that as we undo the chains of the prisoners, share our food with the hungry, bring the homeless into our homes, and give clothes to someone who has none, *then* our light will shine like the dawn, and our wounds will heal quickly.

But I can't give away what I don't have. I myself have to put on the clothes of praise. I have to choose it. I don't know about you, but my clothes don't just jump out of the closet and right onto my body. That would be great; actually, it would be even better if they jumped off of the floor (I admit some of them are there right now!) right onto my body, clean, smelling good, and *ironed!*

I really hate ironing. Just the other day, one of my friends said she loved it—she likes the smell of the steam hitting the clothes or something. Personally, I think she needs prayer! ☺

But back to my point—and I was making one: as children of God, we have His Spirit living inside us, and we need to act like it! We have gladness and joy available to see us through whatever challenges we face. And we need to be able to give it away. Why? Because, ultimately, our job is to help people. We are in the rebuilding-of-lives business!

Hope: Never to Be Hoarded

While Jesus was hanging on the Cross, in agony, feeling isolated and abandoned, He listened to the conversation between two thieves crucified on either side of Him. When one turned to Jesus and asked to be remembered, Jesus assured him that he would see Paradise that very day. In the midst of His own pain and suffering, He took His eyes off His misery and offered encouragement to someone else in pain.

In the midst of your storm . . . be a hope giver.

a happy heart is
good medicine and a
cheerful mind
works healing.
—Old Testament,
Proverbs 17,
verse 22

THREE

LIGHTEN YOUR LOAD

They began to throw the
cargo overboard.

—New Testament, Acts 27,
verse 18 (NIV)

I travel regularly. I have packed suitcases numerous times, but I still take too much. I don't notice it so much when someone else is carrying my bag, but if I have to haul it down the stairs to my car, or up the stairs to the hotel room, I definitely feel the weight. My goal, as I pack, is always to take just enough. But I fail regularly! This is because, as I am packing, I think, *I might need this . . . and this . . . and that.* You never know! Most of the time I don't need whatever it was, so it just becomes extra weight in my bag.

Of course, I can't travel without my laptop, which means I have to bring all of the plugs, attachments, and accessories. I finally got a special backpack just for my computer and all the stuff that comes with it. Great! Now I have another bag to transport. At least this one is on my back, which keeps my hands free to pull my two suitcases. This does seem to work, but I am sure I look very burdened as I make my way through the airport.

One time, after speaking at a conference in Scotland, I was going to take a few days off and see some of the country with some friends. We thought riding the train would be fun. Silly me. I had packed for a multi-day conference, which meant more than one outfit a day. Now, as I was taking my fun days, all my stuff had to come with me. My friends watched as I struggled with very big bags, up and down train platforms. Believe it or not, most of the people on the platform stopped and stared. They looked as if they had never seen anyone with that much luggage. Maybe they hadn't! I have overheard some of my international friends comment on the amount of luggage that Americans travel with. Maybe we just feel more comfortable with lots of stuff!

Another time I was traveling, my suitcases were lost. Well, they weren't lost . . . they went to Des Moines, and I was in Denver. Hope they enjoyed their trip! I did have my makeup and a toothbrush in my carry-on, so all was not lost. I must say that it wasn't nearly as bad as I thought it would be. A girl can go far with a clean pair of underwear and her makeup! And I am not giving up the makeup, no matter what the minimalists say! But I could learn to travel lighter.

The Crew Had a Great Idea

The ship Paul was on carried both passengers and cargo. It had stopped at different ports of call and collected varied goods. Just like those ships at different ports of call, we take on baggage throughout our journey through life. Oftentimes, we don't notice the extra stuff until a storm hits and we have to deal with the things we have dragged on board with us.

Most of us have been betrayed at one point or another in life. If we haven't dealt with it, we carry the baggage of bitterness. Some people are now on their deathbeds, complaining, bitter, unforgiving.

Sometimes, in the face of crisis, we have had to shift into survival mode; we've become overprotective of ourselves and a little distant. In an attempt to be discerning, maybe we've actually become untrusting. In trying to allow ourselves time and space to heal, we've actually become unloving and unavailable. What once helped us to survive is now the baggage that weighs us down—and it can actually sink our boats!

Have you ever been trying to endure your storms only to realize that you are fighting more than one battle? One is the storm you are trying to survive, and the other is the baggage you brought along with you. I'm talking about the trunks and carry-on bags of past hurts, insecurities, and fears.

When you are building a relationship with a new friend, you may encounter some problems that cause you to realize, *Wow, she has some baggage. I don't know if this relationship can work if she doesn't deal with those issues.*

Whether it's cleaning out the garage (yikes—that's a full-time job!), the closet (do I have to?), or the secrets of your soul, the dilemma is the same. How can you tell what you don't need, and what is the good stuff? Have you ever asked yourself as you are doing the cleaning out, *Who gave this to me? And why do I still have it?*

After you live in a home for a year or two and you decide to move, you discover, *I have collected a lot of junk. What can I throw out before I have to rent an eighteen-wheeler?* Sorting through all the "treasures" collected over the years, maybe you discover that there are things that seemed important to you for a while, but now they are just bogging you down.

Most airlines have a limit to the amount of baggage you can take with you. If you want to take more than the allotted amount, they may charge you. (Personally, I think that their idea of what should be allowed is *way* too small . . . but they didn't ask me!) I know about their fees because I have had to pay them more than once! Excess emotional baggage costs you too. It clutters your mind. It drains your energy. It takes away from your ability and energy to deal with what is important.

The crew on Paul's ship had a smart idea for steadying their vessel: they began to toss the excess overboard. We need to do the same with our emotions. To save ourselves— to reach the shore—we have to let go of all that is detrimental to our survival. If you are in the middle of a treacherous storm, this is the time to lighten your load.

> Excess emotional baggage costs you too. It clutters your mind. It drains your energy. It takes away from your ability and energy to deal with what is important.

Can we be really honest for a moment? Look at your past, and see how you've carried some baggage with you that you eventually had to let go of. If you have let go of things before, it helps you to realize that you can do it again.

What baggage do you need to dump today?

Common Baggage Burdens

In a lifetime of working on my heart, and almost twenty years ministering in a local church, I have learned to recognize some common baggage that people carry with them. Some are hidden in expensive Louis Vuitton or Tumi bags, but it is still baggage. Let's take a look at some of the types that I see most often.

PAST HURTS

Past hurts are pains you struggle with today, even though they originate from sometime in your past. The hurt might come from a former marriage, a childhood disappointment, or a tragedy in your teens. You just haven't been able to deal with or fix it yet.

I knew someone who was facing a storm in her dating life. In the midst of the storm, and after getting some help, she realized that she was carrying issues from a disastrous past relationship. A man's actions had hurt her before, so she was projecting all of those qualities onto her new guy. Her excess cargo was about to sink the relationship.

Hurts encompass so much. They can take so much of our

hearts. It's as though each hurt comes with its own set of luggage. Someone once gave me a gift of hand-painted nesting boxes. When I opened the lid, I saw another vessel inside just like it, except littler. And when I took the lid off of that smaller one, there was another. You get the picture. You can stand them in a line, side by side, and each one is just slightly smaller than the next. Painful experiences are like that: each carries its own luggage.

You might carry unforgiveness, and that breeds resentment. Then we realize we have to deal with the bitterness. Next might be envy. You discover you are not willing to trust again. Each piece of luggage involves another one. If we don't lighten our load and intentionally lose some of this stuff, we can spend the rest of our lives crippled by the weight.

Jesus told us that one of the reasons He came was to heal the brokenhearted. So many people are walking around with shattered hearts. Sometimes we try to hide it. We smile, we talk about the things we want to do in our lives, we chat about the latest entertainment news—but inside, we are the walking wounded. Sometimes we feel so much older than our years on this planet, mainly because of the hurts inside us; we're dying just a little bit every day. (And no amount of makeup can hide a broken heart.)

Hurts can be from so many sources. They may come from failures we

I GET THE FEELING JESUS WANTS US TO BE GOLD-MEDAL WINNERS IN THE FORGIVENESS EVENTS.

experienced along the way. They may come from broken relationships with those we once loved so much.

Whatever its source, in order to get rid of the baggage of past pain, we have to be willing to forgive—sincerely, deeply—those who have hurt us. Are you good at forgiving? Sometimes I am. Most of the time, I have to work at it. I get the feeling Jesus wants us to be gold-medal winners in the forgiveness events. Many of us are happy just to try. But to excel in it—to actually let go of the pain—that seems like a lot to ask. I think I'm doing pretty good just not killing someone. ☺

The bottom line is, forgiveness takes practice and determination. Like choosing joy, it requires an act of will. I never *feel* like forgiving. I feel like smacking the person who hurt me! But I don't want this piece of baggage to sink my ship, so I decide to forgive. Daily. Until the pain of the offense goes away.

Choosing forgiveness is like putting medicine on our wounds. The process stings sometimes, but it brings fast, thorough healing.

DISAPPOINTMENTS HURT

The sting of disappointment, in itself, can be as devastating as any violent act. When you have set your heart on something, not achieving it can become a poison that contaminates the very blood that flows through your heart. For example:

- The childless woman just passing forty years of age, who still longs for a baby.

- The man who always wanted to start his own business, who sees that his windows of opportunity are no longer open.

- The teenage girl hoping to be beautiful like the women in magazines, who realizes her body and facial structure are nothing like theirs.

- The young lady with her eyes on a certain career, who fails interview after interview.

To get rid of the baggage of disappointment, we need to replace our distorted views with new vision and expectation. It's natural for our hearts to dream, to believe and hope for wonderful experiences. Hurt and disappointment distort our hope for the future. When we can allow the Holy Spirit to renew our inner pictures of ourselves, our futures, and our God . . . we will be well on our way to carrying less baggage.

FEAR PARALYZES

Another piece of baggage I see so often is fear. Fear is such a debilitating force. It has an amazing power—it magnifies problems. It changes our perception of the world. It can make everything appear worse than it really is, and so negative and hopeless. And then it can cause our fearful view of life to become our realities. A visiting speaker at our church once said, "Fear is the darkroom where negatives are developed."

The symbol for the dramatic arts is two masks: one with a

big smile, and one with tears. Faith and fear are like that. They are like twin brothers who live in the same house. Their voices are similar. They both look something like their parent—you. Sometimes it's difficult to tell one from the other. And they both create power in your life, so where we put our energy and our focus is crucial.

More and more people I have talked to over the years are controlled by fear. People make more decisions out of fear than any other emotion. But we have a choice. We can feed our fear or feed our faith. The one we decide to feed is the one that will flourish. The energy and attention you give to one will diminish the other.

I knew a couple working on their marriage. This was marriage number two for her, and it was looking pretty stormy. When they came to get help, we discovered that the root to the current storm was somewhere in her first marriage. It had been a volatile one, with lots of yelling and fighting. He disappeared whenever things got tough. She came out of that marriage feeling very hurt and afraid.

When she married again, she covered up those emotions: at first, she refused to argue or even to express an opinion. Well, that lasted only a few months, and then, like most of our marriages, the differences surfaced and the confrontation started. Rather than deal with any of it, she just withdrew. She thought if she just didn't say anything, this marriage would be okay. She didn't want this husband to disappear when they argued the way the first one had.

The thing is, this husband had no intention of disappearing. He wanted to work on their marriage, and he didn't understand why she wouldn't talk. When it all came to light, she began to deal with her fear. She realized that it would sink her marriage if she held on to it.

You are painting the picture of your life. The energy you give one—either faith or fear—will color your world and create the emotional accents of the painting you are creating. Which color do you want to add to your masterpiece, faith or fear?

Letting go of the baggage of fear takes a determined desire to focus on the promises of God. David said we should "magnify the LORD." To me, the meaning of "magnify" is simple: Make God big. Make His promises larger than life. Magnify them until they are larger than the problems we are facing.

His promises are inspiring. They encourage us when we apply them to our individual circumstances. They can drastically affect our attitudes when they become our personal sources of hope.

We magnify His promises by reading His Word, memorizing Scriptures, talking about them, and singing songs that build faith. The real world—His world—becomes our reality more than the threat of any imposing destruction to our lives.

INSECURITY HINDERS

You are an important instrument in the plan of God. He has created you out of the inspiration of His love. He has designed you to enjoy a life of fulfillment and significance. Yet, somehow we have allowed our experiences in life, the comments of others, and our feelings to shape our views of ourselves, and we often have so little confidence in who we are.

The writer of Hebrews told us not to "throw away [our] confidence; it will be richly rewarded." God created us with amazing ability and potential, yet so many of us are riddled with questions like . . .

- *Am I important?*

- *Do I have what it takes to make a difference?*

- *Do others value me and my contributions?*

- *Can I be accepted and respected if I am myself?*

When, at the cores of our souls, these questions come to us, our insecurities have no answer to offer. At best, we may meekly whisper, "I hope so."

A three-eyed monster lurks within this piece of baggage; his name is Insecurity, Insufficiency, and Insignificance. He is the Goliath in our lives. He stands tall, mocking and threatening. His victims are obvious and numerous.

Insufficiency shouts: "You don't have enough education, money, or talent. You don't have enough faith. Someone *like* you could possibly accomplish something, but not you. You have *almost* enough skill. If you had just a bit more experience or time or friends or talent or . . . Nope, let's be honest here: you just aren't up to the challenge."

Insignificance chimes in, "If you were taller, nicer, or even stronger—maybe. But you aren't. And no one really needs you. You are not that important to the team. You are not right for the part. You aren't enough."

Insecurity is the result. He whispers, "Well, you did fail that other time. It probably is true—you can't do this, either. Your God cannot help you. You are going to lose, and you should just accept it. Be careful that you don't think you are more important than you are. It is time to surrender to what you secretly suspected all along."

David faced Goliath with a far greater picture of God, faith in his heart, and a song in his mouth. My husband has said, "The army of Israel thought Goliath was too big to fight, but David thought, *He's too big to miss.*'"

In this story we read that David ran "quickly" to Goliath. When Joshua and Caleb faced giants in the promised land, they still went back and told the others that they needed to go "at once" to claim their inheritance. It is not good to look at what you fear for too long. Staring at the storm won't eliminate fear; you will only begin to feel insecure, thinking that you can never get through the situation.

God said I am wonderfully made. I am His masterpiece. I have value. In fact, He says my value is "far above rubies or pearls." You and I are His daughters, which makes us princesses. It is crucial that we understand that we are the glorious, delightful, irreplaceable, irresistible, loved-beyond-measure daughters of the King. As His masterpieces, He has created us with specific strengths and abilities to do His work on the earth. When we don't understand this, we will carry the baggage of insecurity around . . . and this cargo will sink us in any storm. Rather than admitting that we are unsure of ourselves, we will attack others who are bold. Their confidence exposes our insecurity.

I knew a couple of women—we'll call them Jenny and Gaby—whose friendship was growing . . . and then they encountered a storm. While she wouldn't admit it at first, Gaby was jealous of Jenny. Most things seemed to come easy to Jenny: achieving at school, finding a husband, having children, building a successful career. The truth is, Jenny worked as hard as anyone to gain what she enjoyed in life—nothing had fallen out of the sky. But to Gaby, it just didn't seem fair. She couldn't even find a nice guy to date. Her biological clock was ticking. She felt unsatisfied at work, never believing she was doing a good job. She tried to be happy about Jenny's new promotion, but Jenny could tell that it wasn't genuine, and so she began to pull away from the friendship.

> IT IS CRUCIAL THAT WE UNDERSTAND THAT WE ARE THE GLORIOUS, DELIGHTFUL, IRREPLACEABLE, IRRESISTIBLE, LOVED-BEYOND-MEASURE DAUGHTERS OF THE KING.

When I talked to Gaby, we realized that Jenny wasn't the first friend with whom she'd had problems. Her feelings of inadequacy and insecurity had produced jealousy again and again, and she lost friends because of it.

When we lack confidence, when we are wrestling with insecurity, we will be unstable and anxious about many areas of life. Our feelings of insecurity will destroy relationships.

To begin to erase such feelings, change the picture you now have of yourself, and begin to see yourself as the masterpiece of your Creator. Yes, it takes work, and insecurity can be a heavy bag to throw overboard. But if you are going to reach the shore, you must.

Have you ever encountered someone with a major attitude? Okay, that's a dumb question. Maybe it should be: How many people have you seen with a bad attitude . . . today? We often walk away from such folks muttering to ourselves, "What's wrong with that guy?" (Or "that girl" . . . but just not as often!)

When someone has a bad attitude, it is so often the result of one of these pieces of baggage. The attitude is the fruit of carrying that weight around. Instead of joy or love or peace, we see stress, anxiety, or just being uptight.

The apostle Peter gave us some great advice when he told us to give all our worries and cares to God. Well, David tells us to pile our troubles on God's shoulders— He'll carry our loads, He'll help us out.

GOD INVITES US TO PUT OUR LOAD ON HIM. IT'S AN EXCHANGE PROGRAM. WE TRADE OUR LOAD FOR HIS— AND HIS LOAD IS LIGHT.

What a picture. God invites us to put our load on Him. It's an exchange program. We trade our load for His—and His load is light. Good deal!

GIVE IT UP—ALL OF IT

There is a story of a man walking along a lonely, dusty road. He had a large and heavy bag thrown over his shoulder. Despite this, he patiently put one foot in front of the other as he made his journey down the road. The man looked as though his bag was pulling him into the ground as he slowly walked under its burden.

Another man happened by, riding in a horse-drawn wagon. Stopping alongside the traveler, he asked, "Would you like a ride?" Grateful, the weary traveler hopped up into the wagon, relieved to have someone to help him on his journey.

But to the amazement of the driver, the old passenger refused to let go of his valuable baggage. He continued to hold the heavy load over his shoulder as he sat in the wagon. The stranger enjoyed some relief—he didn't have to walk anymore. But he still bore his burden.

It doesn't really make sense, does it? But don't we do that sometimes? We have a God who loves us and cares for us and wants to carry our load, but we are only partially willing to trust Him with the burdens of our lives. We are not designed to carry that baggage. It will keep us from doing what He created us to do. It will make us vulnerable to the storms of life. Yet often we are willing to allow Him to carry only some of the concerns of our lives.

Lose Those Encumbrances

Allow me to veer off of the ship-and-storm analogy and paint another picture. The writer of Hebrews pleaded with us to strip off and "throw aside every encumbrance (unnecessary weight) . . . [and] run with patient endurance . . . the appointed course of the race that is set before us." This reminds me of the Olympics. I like watching all of the events—well, almost all of them. I do have a hard time with the boxing! But I love the track and field competitions, seeing men and women pushing their bodies to the limits of speed and endurance. I must say, I have never seen an Olympic runner try to compete in a race with weights strapped to him or her. I have never seen any of them attempt to run a race with a ball and chain strapped to their leg or while carrying suit-cases. Yet, many of us are trying to get to our finish line carrying lots of bags. Won't work.

It's time to pile our burdens on Him. Drop the baggage—all of it—that can sink you.

Lord Jesus, When You rode into Jerusalem on Palm Sunday, You knew it was the road to the cross, Yet still you took that road. Give me the courage to take the road I should today, Whatever it may mean, wherever it may lead. May I travel trustfully and obediently through this day, content to leave tomorrow in Your safe hands, and tonight rest in Your peace. — Margaret Cundiff

I always told God, "I'm going to hold steady on You, an' You've got to see me through."
—Harriet Tubman

FOUR

PRIORITIES MATTER

*They threw out with their own
hands the ship's equipment
(the tackle and the furniture).*

—New Testament,
Acts 27, verse 19

Tackle and furniture are nice things to have on a journey, but when the situation is life or death, we had better get rid of the stuff we don't really need.

I recently saw the movie *Pirates of the Caribbean*. In one scene, a ship's crew was trying to outrun an attacking pirate ship. They were sailing for their lives. They realized that the pirate ship was faster and was catching up. So in order to escape it they began to throw everything that wasn't nailed down overboard. Soon barrels of food, boxes of supplies, and furniture were floating in the Caribbean. (I'm not going to tell you what happened. You might want to see the movie!!)

The question is: What are your real priorities? We've already seen that, if you are in the middle of a storm, you need to eliminate the extra cargo that is slowing you down. To help us determine what stays and what goes over the side, we need to decide what our true priorities are.

Actually, we should be living by priorities all the time—not just thinking about them when things get rough. Living by priorities needs to be a habit. Living by priorites is living on purpose; this lifestyle can protect our relationships. It will lead us to fulfillment. Being able to determine what your personal priorities are might just save your life.

What Goes, What Stays—and Why

The early pioneers in America moved west in covered wagons. Some movies have made it seem so romantic and adventurous. I don't think so. I think it was probably one of the hardest things ever done! And the smell of that many unwashed bodies . . . not to mention remembering the directions . . . it almost makes me shudder! There were no navigation systems on those wagons. However did they do it?!

Weary families in long lines of wagons filled with supplies and keepsakes made the treacherous journey, day after day, mile after mile. But slowly, poor health, bad weather, lack of food, exhaustion, and battles with Indians who were trying to protect their own land, took their toll.

Lives were lost. Supplies were destroyed. The line of wagons got smaller. For the sake of survival, the pioneers had to throw out some of their possessions. When they had packed for the trip, these items looked like priorities, but now, in the face of death, keepsakes became expendable luxuries. I'm sure they said things like, "That portrait of Grandma is lovely, but since I have to keep the load in the wagon light so that I can go fast, and so if I have to choose between the portrait and food, I'll say good-bye to Grandma!"

They tossed priceless antiques, well-loved books, and large crates of sweet memories—anything that would not help them survive the wilderness. I imagine that there were a few tears as treasures hit the trail. But the pioneers were focused on getting through the rough part and reaching their new home. They had to release everything that did not help them get there.

We should live life asking ourselves, *What's the most important thing?* We can plan our day, focus our efforts, or organize our schedules so that we get those things done first. The other stuff is secondary; not wrong or bad—just not a priority. When you've accomplished the priorities, you can work then on other activities or projects, and they are then acceptable and fun.

Secondary things are frivolous, a waste of time, or just wrong when you have not taken care of priorities. If you have young children at home and are tired of the drudgery, it is not okay to leave the kids at home and take off for six months to travel the globe. Your priority is your children. Later on in life, traveling the globe would be great. It just can't be a priority now. I know this seems obvious, but in my years of ministry I have seen people do the wildest things simply because, in the midst of a storm, they forgot what their priorities were.

Recognizing our real priorities in life can be refreshing and empowering. Some very smart person said, "The main thing is to keep the main thing, the main thing." That's deep. (☺) What we often do is use up the best of our energy on insignificant activities and things, and then find we have nothing left for the priorities. When we are in a storm, we actually have only enough energy for the "main things"!

I can't tell you what your priorities in life should be, but you should figure them out. A couple I talked to said that their marriage was a priority. Great. It should be. But it became clear that they weren't really living as if it were, and they were in a storm because of it. The wife was exhausted, working a full-time job, helping at her children's school, keeping the house fairly tidy, and cooking a meal every day when she got home. The husband wasn't content; he complained that he wanted his wife to have some energy for him at the end of the day (if you know what I mean!).

Well, when we talked, I realized the problem was that she was doing so much during the day, she was exhausted by 7 P.M. (Does this sound like anyone you know??) And he was expecting too much of one overworked woman.

So I asked him what his priority was: having a home-cooked meal every night, a clean house, an extra paycheck, or what? If he wanted her to have the energy and desire to make love a few nights a week, then he was going to have to help: let her stop pouring herself into some of the other areas. If she prioritized time with her husband, she needed to let go some of the energy drainers in her life. They had to determine the key priorities in their married life and make the necessary adjustments.

Now, I am not saying that you can go to your husband and announce, "If you ever want to have sex with me again, you are going to have to hire a maid and a chef." I am saying that we need to look at our priorities, and make sure we are acting accordingly. This couple's marriage had been in a storm simply because they had forgotten what was important.

Sometimes reevaluating our life's meaning and value can be extremely clarifying and freeing. Asking yourself the right questions can be a life-altering exercise. The old question, "If your house caught on fire and you could only save three things, what would they be?" is supposed to help us see what really matters to us. Obviously we should keep all that important stuff in a fire-proof shed out in the backyard! (Yay! I'm going out to buy a shed!)

When the fires raged in southern California, I asked myself that question. Those fires destroyed almost 4,000 homes and 800,000 acres, and one that was out of control was about a mile from my house.

I had to ask myself, *If we are asked to evacuate, what should I take?* (I was grateful that we had an SUV, because I could have filled it up!) The fire turned a different direction, and it was someone in another neighborhood who was asking that question.

And obviously, the most important things in our lives are what we should put our time and focus on—because they truly are what matters. We can't put the same amount of worry or care into small, everyday matters, or we will drive ourselves nuts!

Where to Put Our Energy

My husband, Philip, teaches about a leadership concept called the 80/20 principle. The simple explanation is that 20 percent of your efforts produce 80 percent of the results you want; and 80 percent of your efforts produce 20 percent of the results. If this is accurate, then only 20 percent of the things you focus on bring 80 percent of your fulfillment. The list goes on like this:

- Only 20 percent of the people produce 80 percent of the results.

- Only 20 percent of the sales force sells 80 percent of the product.

- Only 20 percent of the population earns 80 percent of the money.

And so on. The idea is that, once we recognize the 20 percent with the most value and impact, we can put our focus there—because that is where most of our impact will be felt.

This is a great way to evaluate the difference between your effort and your results. Picture a scene in a movie in which a man is on his deathbed. It's probably the last day of his life. Is he concerned that he didn't get to drive the coolest kind of car? I don't think so. Is he wishing he had made one more business deal? Probably not. Is he regretting that he didn't buy one more pair of shoes? (Well . . . okay, maybe the shoes.)

But seriously, I think that most of us would be thinking about our relationships with the ones we love. We would probably look back at our lives to see if we had fulfilled what God put us on the earth to do. Did we make an impact in our communities? Did we matter to people? Are our key relationships in the condition we want them to be in as we leave this earth? Maybe this is where we should be spending our 80 percent.

SORTING THROUGH THE BOMBARDMENT

Jesus gave us some very simple but profound direction. He told us to seek first the kingdom of God. To me that means that our priority, in a storm or on calm seas, should always be what honors God. What will help build His church in our world? What will help us draw others to God? What will help us grow as believers?

> OUR PRIORITY, IN A STORM OR ON CALM SEAS, SHOULD ALWAYS BE WHAT HONORS GOD.

This verse helps us sort through all the options that bombard our thinking. Our emotions and others' desires can distract us. We can lose sight of what we're really here to do.

The Bible gives us some examples of people who knew what their priorities were.

- Two mothers came to King Solomon fighting over one baby. They both claimed to be the mother, saying that the other one had rolled on her own baby in the night and killed it. Solomon, in his wisdom, said that he would cut the baby in half and they could share. The real mother said, "No, give the baby to her." She understood that the priority was that the baby lived, not that she won the battle.

- Three young Hebrew boys, Shadrach, Meshach, and Abednego, were ordered to bow down to the king's idol. They refused, thus incurring his wrath. They knew their priority was not to get the approval of the crowd or the king. They understood, in the midst of their storm, that it was more important to honor God.

- To Jesus, whom religious leaders criticized because He healed a woman on the Sabbath, the priority was to help the sick regardless of what day of the week it was. He understood the importance of a human being, and the unimportance of the calendar.

SIMPLIFY AND INTENSIFY

A basketball coach was meeting with his team at halftime. They had just finished the worst half game they had played all season. They had made many mental errors, and they'd failed to run the plays they spent hours practicing. They were so bad, they looked as if they didn't even know how to play the game, and the score showed it.

The coach looked at his players and just wasn't even sure exactly where to start. He said, "Okay, guys, let's start with the priorities. This orange ball is a basketball. Our first job is to put it into our basket. Second, we want to keep the other team from putting the ball into its basket. I'm not sure what you were trying to do out there, but let's just focus on these two priorities."

Can you imagine Jesus sitting down with us in our locker room and saying, "This is the Bible. These words should guide you in loving God and loving each other. You're getting off track."

One of the instructions I have heard from God so often in life is "Simplify and intensify." In other words, don't overcomplicate your life. Intensify your efforts on the main goals.

If you are in a storm right now, rather than freaking out—which I do upon occasion!—remember what the important things in your life are, and focus on those. Don't let the waves crashing against you distract you from your priorities.

A Game or a Lifestyle?

Trivial Pursuit has been a popular game. It is based on our knowledge of facts and truths that have little impact on our quality of life. I've played that game, and I actually like it (I must confess!). The game is fun; living our lives in pursuit of the trivial is not!

To many people, it's not a game; it's a lifestyle. Sometimes we are more concerned about a celebrity news story than we are about our own ups and downs. Someone else's drama can be so involving, so alluring, that we forget to focus on the priorities of our own lives.

When the military has a target, the target becomes the priority. The emotions, feelings, and attitudes of the military personnel don't sway them from their goal. We could learn a little from this. If my priority is to develop a healthier body, then nothing—not ice cream, chocolate, french fries, or a rainy day—should keep me from reaching my goal.

In pastoring a church, my husband and I are always trying to help people learn to handle relationships effectively. We train our leaders to be careful about being pulled into someone's drama, because once they are, it is easy to lose focus. The expression "He can't see the forest for the trees" means that someone has lost sight of the important and is letting the insignificant confuse him.

Because all of us care about people so much, often we react and run to the rescue, and we hear, "Someone did this or that. He took advantage of me." Jesus told us that if someone offends us, we should go to him and deal with it. But our first reaction is to get involved. We want to arrange a meeting between the two to work it out. If instead we ask, "Did you go to him yourself and discuss it?" more often than not the answer is "No."

The priority for our leaders is to train that person how to handle conflicts in life, not to get involved in his trouble. The offended party should talk to his offender. If he needs help, he can come back and get it. This keeps leaders from being sucked into someone else's priority and allows them to focus on their own. (In the midst of a storm, my own priorities keep me busy enough!)

In my current storm, am I putting my time and energy in the right place? am I focusing on the important things?

The Three Biggies

Our time is so valuable. Our energy is our lives' strength. What are we investing it in? Is it worth it? In my current storm, am I putting my time and energy in the right place? Am I focusing on the important things?

The great apostle Paul, as he was mentoring his son in the faith, told Timothy to remember the main goal. He said that the "goal of our instruction is love from a pure heart and a good conscience and a sincere faith." Look at Paul's priority list: every one of our goals or investments should be building one of these three areas, or it is simply not a priority.

- Love from a pure heart

- A good conscience

- Sincere faith

Ask yourself: Does this project I am pursuing build one of these areas in my life? Will this class help produce love, faith, or a good conscience in me? Does this issue I'm focusing on help build one of these elements in anyone's life? While I am navigating a storm, am I keeping these issues as a priority in my heart?

Let's look at each of these priorities more closely.

ALL YOU NEED IS LOVE

In the middle of the storms in my life, I can't forget what life is all about—love. I must be living by the principles of love to survive the dark clouds and waves. I have to be living under the influence of love to win the battles of life.

A Pharisee asked, "Teacher, which is the most important commandment in the Law of Moses?" Jesus replied, " 'You must love the Lord your God with all your heart, all your soul, and all your mind.' This is the first and greatest commandment. A second is equally important: 'Love your neighbor as yourself.' "

That's what priorities are all about: loving God and loving people. Let's keep it simple. Are you going through a storm right now? Don't lose your love for God. It's a priority. We can't do life with joy and fulfillment without God. Hold on to your love for Him. Pursue His love. So many make the mistake of throwing out the most important aspect of life—a relationship with God. His love is not expendable. In responding to the battles of life, don't run from God. Run to Him.

In the midst of the trial you might be in, keep loving the people in your world. I know it is easy to get frustrated with them—especially when the waves are crashing against you. When work or school or a friendship is tough, remember that the people in your world are the priority. Just go home and love on your family . . . or go out with your girlfriends. People are always more important than things or situations. In the midst of our crises, we must remember that.

One time I was visiting a young woman in the hospital, who had been diagnosed with a life-threatening disease. She was married and had a young child. The diagnosis had shocked her and her husband. But when I entered the hospital room, they were playing with their daughter. We had some time to chat, and I encouraged them . . . but honestly, they seemed to be handling it. Was she afraid? I'm sure. Was he worried about losing his wife? You bet. But in the midst of their storm, they were loving each other and leaning on God. They were loving and laughing. What a way to get through a storm. An inspiration to me.

a GOOD CONSCIENCE

One of God's priorities is to bring healing to our souls. He wants to free us from guilt and shame and establish peace of mind. I believe that God wants to bring joy to our lives. Enjoying genuine peace and joy are signs of the "good conscience" that Paul wrote about.

The storms we ride out are difficult enough without having to deal with guilt and shame as well. We have the incredible privilege of confessing our sins and weaknesses to the Father and being forgiven. Then we can sail through the storm with clean consciences. As you are working through your tough situation, keep in mind that everything you do should leave you with a good conscience.

I have made some bad decisions in my life. I know that's a shock to you! Recently, I was preparing a women's event in a new location. We had a bigger budget than I had worked with before, and I was really being stretched. Someone made a mistake, and because of that we failed to promote the event—and that left us headed to a new city with a great program, but no audience. I was in a storm . . . with very little time to fix it.

I knew I should have stayed a little more connected to our office, to the team, to the person involved. I just thought I could handle it. Pride. Not good. Now we were faced with a mistake that could cost us thousands. I was in a storm with a mind full of guilt, wondering how I could have handled it better.

To get through this storm, I knew I needed a clear conscience. There is only one way to get that: repentance! I talked to God and asked Him to forgive me for my pride, and I made sure I connected myself to the team and the office better. Peace filled me, and I knew I would reach the shore. (The lesson wasn't over, however; you'll see what else I learned, a few pages ahead!)

One of the most amazing stories Jesus told was of the prodigal son. When the boy realized he needed to return to his father, he didn't feel worthy of being his father's son. So many people walk through life, feeling that deep sense of unworthiness— whether due to failures they experienced or just a conclusion they have reached in their own minds. The father in this story, upon hearing about the repentance of his son, responded by embracing him and throwing a party. He let his son see he was glad he was home. He not only accepted the boy, but he let him know that he was important.

It is a priority that we keep our mind free from attacks from within that would keep us from having a good conscience. Repent if you need to . . . and keep a strong and positive attitude about who God has made you!

SINCERE FAITH

A sincere faith is genuine trust in God. It is a faith that affects how we live every day of the week. It is a faith that we can apply to our real-life situations. Learn all of the theology that you want . . . get all of the knowledge you can . . . but make sure that you are not just building a vast reservoir of religious information or trying to be doctrinally superior. Studying the Bible should build a simple, humble, and authentic faith.

I knew some very smart people who had studied the Bible and searched out all sorts of topics and verses. They knew the information; they just didn't seem to know God. When a storm of sickness came into their lives, they wilted, because while they had the knowledge, they didn't have faith in their God to see them through. They kept looking for the intellectual answers. It is not just knowledge that will get you through the storm, but faith in Him.

We show our faith not only in what we believe, but in how we demonstrate it. You should know I am a woman of faith, not only because of what I say, but by the way I live. My faith shouldn't just be evident by how many Bible verses I know, but by how many I am living.

Paul challenged the Corinthians to excel in faith. I read that and asked myself, *Am I getting better at faith? Is my faith genuine? Is it making a difference in my everyday life, or is it merely theological?* I started working on a list of things I ought to know by now, and excelling in faith was one of them. How about you? Are you letting your faith guide your life?

I was watching a music awards show recently and saw a

young man win for one of his songs. While he certainly is talented in his genre of music, in my opinion his particular style is vulgar, crude, and perverted, and it degrades women. The truth is, none of that shocks me; I know all kinds of music are out there. What did shock me was his response upon receiving the award. As he held up his treasure, he began to thank his "Lord and Savior, Jesus Christ."

How sad. Maybe he should ask for Jesus' help the next time he writes a song!! There is obviously no integrity between what he believes and how he lives. He is not excelling in faith. Are you? Is the faith you profess evident in your actions?

As I said, my faith could use some work. I find it easy to trust God on the good days, but recently I came face-to-face with my humanity . . . and failed the faith test.

> IT IS NOT JUST KNOWLEDGE THAT WILL GET YOU THROUGH THE STORM, BUT FAITH IN HIM.

I've mentioned the time our God Chick team was planning one of our first really big events, and that the promoter on the team dropped the ball. When I learned this, it was three weeks before the event. I went into the bathroom and cried. You know, the ugly kind of crying, where mascara is running down your cheeks, and your nose is a faucet! Loud and not pretty. I had really wanted this event to be a win for the women on our team, who had volunteered lots of hours, and for the women of the city to which we were headed.

It was a lesson not just in having a good conscience but in

showing a sincere faith. In the midst of my panic, I heard heaven say, "Oh, so your faith was in the promoter, and not in Me?"

I quietly sucked in my breath, and I began to cry again. These were tears of sorrow, because I had let my God down. I had focused on the wind and waves, not on my Father, who had given me what I needed to get to shore. I hadn't had faith in Him. He had called me to go to this city, so of course He would do what was necessary. I apologized to God. I put on some worship music and began declaring who He is. I magnified Him and not my storm. I built up my faith again.

It wasn't long before I was a new woman—with my faith level much fuller. We had some work to do, scrambling to get the promotional materials out there, but we did it. And the event ended up being *amazing!* Hundreds of women attended, and we continue to get e-mails about how the message changed lives. I stand in awe of my God. And I am committed to becoming excellent in faith!

Without a simple faith, not only is it impossible to please Him, but it will be very hard to endure when gale-force winds blow. Make faith a priority! In the middle of the storms, focus on loving, creating a good conscience, and building a sincere faith.

The Bottom Line

A speaker asked for volunteers to help illustrate a point. After gathering the three innocent victims in the front of the room, he gave them their role: "You are all firemen. Your job is to put out fires." Then he explained that since there were no fires today, he was going to give each one a responsibility. "Volunteer One, wash the truck. Number Two, mop the floor. And Number Three, wrap up the hoses neatly."

He had them mime their particular jobs, poked fun at them, and demanded that they act out their imaginary tasks better. It was funny, and we had a lot of laughs. Then he asked each of them, "What was your job again?" Each gave his response, dreading what the speaker might ask them to do next: "Wash the truck." "Mop the floor." "Wrap up the hoses."

Then he drove home his point. "No. You are all wrong. Your job is to put out fires." He had deliberately put all the focus on the other tasks by challenging them to be better actors and put more effort into their responsibilities. Each volunteer and the audience had forgotten what the real job and priority was: to put out fires.

In life, we can lose momentum and fulfillment when we allow things, whether good and interesting or bad and destructive, to slowly and subtly become priorities. In a storm, remembering our lives' priorities is a matter of survival.

Give thanks to the Lord, for He is good! Old Testament, Psalm, Chapter 107, Verse 1a

Time is like loose change. It is given to us here below to buy the real things of eternity. Let us use it!
—Saint Julie Billiart

FIVE

DROP THOSE ANCHORS

They dropped four anchors
from the stern and kept wishing
for daybreak to come.

—NEW TESTAMENT,
ACTS 27, VERSE 29

In the weeks and months after the earthquake, Philip and I got very tired of our earth moving. We decided we wanted to live in a place where the ground stayed still. (Like somewhere in the middle of the country . . . at least with hurricanes and tornadoes, you get some kind of warning!) We were still battling fear with every tremor. So, we thought we should move. I remember praying and asking God what He thought, but honestly, our own emotions got in the way of His voice.

Sometimes that happens. When you are in a storm, your own emotions can take over—which usually isn't a good thing. I thank God I have emotions—I just need to make sure they don't lead me. It's embarrassing to admit that we actually visited different cities, looking for one we thought might make a good home. We didn't really tell anyone; we were too busy trying to chart a new course in the middle of our storm.

Those midnight moments, when we can't see the shore and the storm is raging, it is NOT the time to set a new course. I understand feeling like you need to do something—fix the situation—but making irreversible decisions in the middle of a storm can bring about a whole new one. Philip and I came to our senses and stayed put. I actually cringe now to think of what we almost did. Not that there aren't great places in our country to plant a church . . . they just aren't great places for us. Our destiny lies in Los Angeles . . . earthquakes and all! We could have messed up the plans God had for us by moving.

Our church has grown by more than two thousand people since 1994. Hundreds have begun real relationships with God. We have had the chance to make a significant impact in our city by demonstrating racial harmony and using all of the creative elements this city has to offer. God is doing an amazing thing in our hometown . . . and we almost walked away. We almost changed course.

> Those midnight moments, when we can't see the shore and the storm is raging, it is not the time to set a new course.

Stand Still—and Hang On

Whatever storm you are facing, now is the time to drop anchors and hang on, no matter what you might be feeling. Robert

Schuller wrote:

> The most dangerous thing in the world is to make an irreversible negative decision during a brownout time. Don't sell your real estate because there is no electricity in the building. It's just a brownout, not a burnout. Never cut a dead tree down in the wintertime. I remember one winter my dad needed firewood, and he found a dead tree and sawed it down. In the spring to his dismay new shoots sprouted around the trunk. He said, "I thought sure it was dead. The leaves had all dropped in the wintertime. It was so cold that twigs snapped as surely as if there were no life left in the old tree. But now I see that there was still life at the taproot." He looked at me and said, "Bob, don't forget this important lesson. Never cut a tree down in the wintertime." Never make a negative decision in the low time. Never make your most important decisions when you are in your worst mood.[1]

A woman I knew with young children recently went through a divorce. She was definitely in a storm, just working through all of the emotions that a divorce brings. I know she wanted to change everything; we all do when we are making a new life. She asked for my input in how to handle what she was dealing with. I encouraged her strongly to keep everything the same, as best she could: the children's schools, home, her job, and church. I recommended that she drop anchor until she could see the shore.

Making dramatic decisions just isn't the best thing to do while a storm is still raging.

The Anchors That Will Keep You Afloat

The crew on Paul's ship dropped four anchors. Here are the four I think we should all drop when we are in rough seas.

ANCHOR 1: PURPOSE

When the winds are tossing us in every direction, we can easily lose our way if we don't understand our purpose in life. God created you and me for a purpose. We are not just here to suck in air. We are not exploded tadpoles randomly placed on Earth. No. We are the abundantly loved-beyond-measure daughters (and sons!) of the King, created to fulfill an awesome purpose on this planet. At the end of my life, I don't want people just to say that I paid all of my bills on time, kept a clean house, made a great peanut butter sandwich, and obeyed all of the traffic laws. Well, someone *can* say those things—because they are all good—but surely God put me here for more than that!

God's purpose for us doesn't change. As we grow and mature, the plan gets more refined, but it doesn't change. Sometimes, however, in the midst of a storm, because our world is dark and chaotic, we can make bad decisions that indicate we have forgotten our purpose.

We all have the same general purpose . . . to love God with everything we are, and to love our neighbors as ourselves. But the specifics of how we work that out are what make us unique. Also, according to Proverbs 31, we are all to bring justice and mercy to the planet. We are to speak for those unable to speak for themselves. That is the big picture. We fulfill it every day by giving to and loving those who come across our paths.

Part of my purpose on the planet is to be an encourager and motivator of women. My style of teaching can be fun and inspiring, but not all see it that way. (I know . . . what a shock!) Sometimes women, perhaps out of their own insecurity, attack and criticize what I am doing. They are the spectators. In life there are always more spectators than players. There are more people in the grandstands than there are players on the field, mainly because there is only one requirement to sit in the grandstand: being critical. While we are in the stands, we all think *we* could have made that goal, shot that basket, or been safe at the base. It is easy to be critical when we are not in the game.

If we listen to too much criticism, we can find ourselves in a storm of doubt. I am open to correction from God and a handful of people to whom I am accountable. I just have to close off criticism from others, or I can find myself doubting the purpose of my life, wondering if I do have anything good to offer my generation. I start to question whether I should do something else. Being in front of people makes me easy to shoot at, so I think, *I don't want to be target practice for others. Maybe I should give up on the woman thing and become a professional golfer* (Not a chance, by the way!) *or just sit in the back of church where I can't feel the arrows.* Just like you, I have to remind myself of my purpose, so I drop that anchor and stay the course.

> **WHAT WE DO COMES OUT OF WHO WE ARE, NOT THE OTHER WAY AROUND.**

Another part of the purpose of my life is to be a mother. Most of the time, I love being Mom. Some moments, however, it is very hard. When I am in the midst of correcting my children, I feel as if the storm is raging. The older my children get, the more challenging and emotionally exhausting the discipline can be. (Anyone relating to this??)

I know women whose older children have gotten involved in pornography, or got caught cutting school or driving without a license. All of these require correction. I'm sure these women felt that handling these problems was like midnight in the middle of a storm. Perhaps it would have been easier for them to just throw up their hands in frustration, give up, and emotionally withdraw from their children. Many parents do. But these women didn't because they were aware of their purpose, which includes being good parents. Even though the storm was raging, they dropped anchor and stayed put.

In the movie *The Patriot,* an English soldier brutally killed one of Ben Martin's sons. Ben wanted to seek revenge. Understandable. He had to be reminded a few times to stay the course. Personal revenge would not help win the Revolution, and that was an even bigger cause than his personal vendetta. In the midst of the storm, Ben almost forgot his purpose. If we are going to make it to shore, we must hang on to God's plan . . . we must drop that anchor!

In his book *First Things First*, author Stephen Covey wrote about Victor Frankl, an Austrian psychologist who survived the concentration camps of Nazi Germany. Frankl made a startling discovery about why some overcame the horrible conditions and some did not.

> He looked at several factors—health, vitality, family structure, intelligence, survival skills. Finally, he concluded that none of these factors was primarily responsible. The single most significant factor, he realized, was a sense of future vision—the impelling conviction of those who were to survive that they had a mission to perform, some important work left to do. Survivors of POW camps in Vietnam and elsewhere have reported similar experiences: a compelling, future-oriented vision is the primary force that kept many of them alive.[2]

Another aspect of purpose is knowing not just what you are on the planet to do, but who you are. What we do comes out of who we are, not the other way around.

In the midst of their storm, the American revolutionaries in 1776 knew who they were. They wrote it like this:

> When in the Course of human Events, it becomes necessary for one People to dissolve the Political Bands which have

connected them with another, and to assume among the Powers of the Earth, the separate and equal Station to which the Laws of Nature and Nature's God entitle them, a decent Respect to the Opinions of Mankind requires that they should declare the causes which impel them to the Separation.

> IT'S THROUGH OUR CREATOR'S EYES THAT WE GET A TRUE PICTURE OF WHO WE ARE.

We hold these Truths to be self-evident, that all Men are created equal, that they are endowed by their Creator with certain unalienable Rights, that among these are Life, Liberty, and the pursuit of Happiness.[3]

They separated themselves from whom they used to be and declared who they were. We need to do the same! Separate ourselves from who we were, and declare who we are now! So, who are we, and where do we get our identity? We don't get it from our driver's licenses; most of the stuff on those is embellished anyway! (Be honest . . . how much does yours say you weigh?) We don't get it from our passports; those just tell us where we've been. We don't get our identity from school report cards; most of us are still dealing with the negative things some teachers said. We don't find out who we are from mirrors; we just use them to put on makeup.

You and I get our identity from our Creator. It's through our Creator's eyes that we get a true picture of who we are.

We are:

- Not victims, but conquerors—in fact, more than conquerors.

- Not losers, but winners.

- Not addicts, but overcomers.

- Not captives, but free people.

- Not sinners, but forgiven.

- Not random creations, or our parents' "accidents," but persons placed on the earth "for such a time as this."

As a daughter of the King, I need to remember I have a crown on my head. I am royalty . . . not to be served, but to serve. All of that is who I am. And in the midst of the storm, I had better keep this in mind, or I will lose my way.

I have written my own declaration—not of independence, but of freedom.

In the course of my life, it has become necessary to dissolve the bands that have tied me to my past and to assume the powers God has entitled to me. I hold these truths to be self-evident: I have been created in the image of God and have bold access to Him at all times. I am His daughter and have all the privileges that come with royalty—I am forgiven, loved unconditionally, free from guilt and shame, healed, and destined for a life of purpose and prosperity. I am set apart to bring life and joy to a hurting world, and I have the courage to do so!

Know who you are in Him. Your ability to fight, to make it through the storm, comes when you do! Jesus said that if we don't have real roots, if we are not grounded, then when (not if, but when!) affliction or trouble or persecution comes, we will stumble.

We will stop trusting God and His plans for us. I don't want to be one who stumbles through life, so I better make sure I know who and Whose I am.

> I DON'T WANT TO BE ONE WHO STUMBLES THROUGH LIFE, SO I BETTER MAKE SURE I KNOW WHO AND WHOSE I am.

Rick Warren said it this way: "God was thinking of you long before you ever thought about him. His purpose for your life predates your conception. He planned it before you existed, *without your input!* You may choose your career, your spouse, your hobbies, and many other parts of your life, but you don't get to choose your purpose."[4] Out of our relationship with God, our job is to discover it.

ANCHOR 2: A CHURCH HOME

In my years of pastoring and leading in church, I have seen people, when they are in storms, run from church rather than to it. Maybe they are embarrassed that they are experiencing such deep difficulty . . . stupid, because we all go through it. Actually, that makes me sad. The house of God should be the first place someone goes when she is hurting. When you are in a storm, don't avoid church—drop anchor there!

Recently I was to speak at a church in Sydney. I had taken my daughter, Paris, with me on the trip, and she and I were driven to the church. (When I am in that country, they drive me around. I guess because they don't want a crazy American on the wrong side of the road!) Before the car had even stopped, Paris hopped out and ran into the building. I yelled out the window, "Where are you going?"

"I'm going to work in the nursery."

"Maybe you should ask someone where it is!" I cried as she disappeared into the building.

She had never been in that church, but as far as she was concerned, she was home. What she did in her own church was help out in the nursery, so, of course, she would do that in Australia as well. I am very glad that she is comfortable in the house of God—no matter in what country she finds herself! I always want her to feel that way, because maybe when she is in a storm one day, her natural response will be to run to God and His people.

I love the house of God. I think it should be the most creative, energetic, loving, awesome place on the earth. So does God. Yes, it is full of imperfect people on a journey, but it should be our number-one destination when we hit any storm. It is the vehicle God uses to establish His kingdom of love on the earth. The "church of the living God . . . is the pillar and support of the truth."

Maybe you have encountered, instead of unconditional love, judgment and criticism in the house of God. I am sorry. A banner hanging in the lobby of our church says, "Welcome Home," because we honestly want it to be a place where the lost, confused, and hurting come in and get help. Home should be a place where you recover and find refreshment.

If you are in church leadership, I challenge you to create such an atmosphere in your church that when the hurting people in your community are in the midst of storms, they can come to your churches and feel welcome—as if they were home.

You and I constitute "the church." The church is definitely not a building, but when we (flesh and blood) gather to the building, it suddenly becomes "the House of God." When we leave and the lights go out, it is merely a building again, but while we are there it becomes the House of God. This House has the capacity to be magnificent, wonderful, and awesome. It has the capacity to carry an anointing from above that can fulfill all of His purposes in all of our lives, and it has the capacity to make a difference in the world.

So many Christians fall short of their potential because they allow themselves to have a casual relationship with their church, not realizing that they are actually family . . . designed to do life together.[5] The truth is, we who are believers all share the responsibility to gather ourselves in the local church, and then plant ourselves there, so that we can flourish. That's what the Bible says. If you want to thrive throughout life, make sure you have roots in the house of God. Don't just visit . . . stay. Drop your anchor. And then, help make it an incredible place full of love and warmth. Help make it a home.

We are to "dwell" in the house of God, as the psalmist says. What does "dwell" mean? Well, it means that we "do life" in the house of God. We don't just show up for mealtimes, then run out the door. At the Wagner house, my family definitely pops in when dinner is on the table; but they also contribute to the running of our home. We all have chores to make home a great place to be. We spend time together. We talk. My husband and I help with homework. I get a hand with the dishes (on a good day!). We hug . . . laugh . . . cry . . . sing . . . work. All of this happens in our home; I think it should happen in the house of God too.

Pick an area of church life and help. If you can sing in key through an entire song (never happens for me), think about the choir. If you can smile, how about being a greeter at the door? If you love children—at least most of the time!—help in the children's ministry. How about computers—can you work them? Maybe the office could use a volunteer. Find an area of service and give. It's all a part of dwelling in the House.

Be present when the doors are open. Don't just tolerate the church service. Smile at people. Hey, maybe the pastor will say something great today . . . take notes! Don't make church a place where you spend an hour on Sunday. Make it a place where you *dwell*. It should be a place where real people with real lives and real problems can find real aid as they worship a real God. It shouldn't just be a place where we get our theological questions answered, but a place where we do life!

Philip and I have gotten so many letters over the years from people who came to us in the midst of a storm. They connected with people in the church, and that helped them make it safely to shore.

Dear Philip and Holly,

I was invited to your church by a friend and decided to come. I guess she could see that my life was in chaos! I was convinced that divorce from my husband was the only option. Our marriage truly was a disaster. But, we came to the church, broken hearts and all, and began to learn how to be champions. We have made friends we will have for years to come. We learned how to build a healthy marriage. Thank you for what you give of yourselves every day . . . Thank you for making this church a place where hurting people can come in and get help.

Dear Philip and Holly,

I came to the church a total mess although I wasn't willing to admit that I was. I have been dealing with issues in my heart that came from being sexually abused as a child. Because of all of this, many aspects of my life were not great. When I walked into the church for the first time I felt like I was home . . . only to one of the first good ones I had ever experienced. It took me a while to understand the unconditional love of God, but I did feel loved and cared for. I began a relationship with Jesus that was more than religion . . . it has changed my life. I met people who truly seemed to care. I was then free to work on the issues of my heart. Thank you for loving, thank you for demonstrating His love to me. I am so grateful for this church and the people I now call family.

In the midst of your storm, make sure you drop anchor—plant yourself—in the house of God. You will grow, make friends who can help you reach shore, and encounter the God who calms troubled seas.

ANCHOR 3: COURAGE

It takes courage to live out our purpose on the planet, and it takes courage to make it through the storms of life.

Courage is not limited to the grand actions of a few. Courage is not just facing the enemy on a battlefield, although many men and women of our nation are doing that now. Courage is not just accomplishing amazing feats of physical strength, such as lifting a car off a trapped victim or escaping locked chains while submerged in an ice bath (!). Courage is finishing the race even if you are in last place. Courage is standing up to your daughter when she wants to go out with the boy who may be "cool," but who you know is dangerous. Courage is having an honest talk with your children about the mistakes of your

> COURAGE IS FINISHING THE RACE EVEN IF YOU ARE IN LAST PLACE.

past so that they won't go down those roads. Courage is forgiving your friend when she lets you down. Courage is loving your husband in the midst of a financial crisis.

What if you have made plans with your girlfriends to do some fun things? You have worked hard and need this time to play. And then your son comes home from school having had a *bad* day . . . flunked a test . . . a friend let him down. Courage is choosing to be selfless and spend time with your son. What if your hairdresser friends don't report the tips they receive on their taxes, and they tell you that you don't have to either? Courage is doing the right thing even if you are the only one.

Courage is refusing to let cancer steal your joy. My friend Sandy was diagnosed with a life-threatening desease. What I saw in her was courage. She faced lots of pain with both the disease and the treatments. Her prognosis was not great. But I saw her handle it all with such class. She is a true woman of faith, and she continually believed God for a miracle. She was not afraid to die—she just would rather not! She was in a serious storm yet had the courage to believe God . . . rather than blame Him.

It does take strength and bravery to trust Him when the waves of the storm are crashing around you. Between the treatments and the hand of God, Sandy got her miracle. I think a big part of it was her courage to believe, to hang on even though the odds were against her.

It takes courage to do something others consider foolish. If you are in a financial storm, don't stop giving! If you have been hurt in relationships—and we all have—it will be tough to keep your heart open. We can all get better at choosing whom we trust, and at how quickly we share our lives with someone; but we do need to be willing to try again. Drop that anchor of courage, or you will find yourself floundering in the middle of the sea.

When our church started, only about ten people attended. It was actually very discouraging. It was winter in L.A., and we froze in the school auditorium in which we held services. (Okay, to the rest of the country, it might not have been cold, but our blood has gotten very thin from living here!) It was disheartening to pour our hearts out to such a small crowd that never seemed to grow.

My parents came to visit and felt our pain. It was a storm. We knew what God had asked us to do; we just had to have the courage to keep going even though it looked like it might not work. When I was in school, I heard someone say that Rosa Parks, who was one of the catalysts of the civil rights movement, said that "knowing what needs to be done does away with fear." We knew what needed to be done. Well-meaning people told us that maybe we should try something else. But we dropped our anchor of courage and hung on.

Now the church has thousands of members. Some theological students have come to our church to study its growth, and they always ask us why we think the church has expanded this way. The first thing we say is that we had the courage to keep on going. A lot of great men and women, who were much smarter than we were, started churches when we did, and a lot of them are no longer around. Our secret? We had the courage to weather the storm.

Ignace Jan Paderewski, the famous Polish composer-pianist, was once scheduled to perform at a great American concert hall for a high-society extravaganza. In the audience was a mother with her fidgety nine-year-old son. Weary of waiting, the boy slipped away from her side, strangely drawn to the Steinway on the stage. Without much notice from the audience, he sat down at the stool and began playing "Chopsticks." Then the crowd began to shout, and hundreds yelled, "Get that boy away from there!"

When Paderewski heard the uproar backstage, he grabbed his coat and rushed out to the stage. Reaching around the boy from behind, the master began to improvise a countermelody to "Chopsticks." As the two of them played together, Paderewski kept whispering in the boy's ear, "Keep going. Don't quit, son, don't stop, don't stop." Together, the master and the novice transformed a frightening experience into a wonderfully creative one. The audience was enthralled.

Whatever the situation, however stormy the seas and dark the night, remember that God is with you and is whispering deep within, "Don't quit. Keep going." Courage isn't the absence of fear, it is not quitting in spite of it.[6]

It takes courage to keep going when all looks hopeless around you. It takes courage to stick it out when so many quit. But courage lives within you—you are the warrior chick! You rise in the midst of adversity—you are not the one who wilts! You are the bold one, staying strong even in difficult times!

David, after Samuel had anointed him to be king but before he actually assumed the throne, was off in the hills developing his army of "mighty men." Actually, he was learning to be a mighty man too. It was the season of sheepshearing (a party time), and David and his men were in the hills above the ranch of a very wealthy man named Nabal. Nabal, whose name means "fool," (what kind of mother chose that name??) was married to Abigail.

While David and his men were in the hills, they were protecting Nabal's sheep and shepherds. Eventually David and his men ran out of supplies. He sent some of his men to Nabal's ranch to give greetings and to ask for some food (an appropriate request in those days). Nabal, certainly not the wisest of men, had had a little too much to drink, and he not only refused the request for food, but cursed David and all of David's family.

What was he thinking?? David was not afraid of killing people. This was David—a man for whom God fought! David's men returned to him and told him all that Nabal had said. Being a man of war, David said, "Strap on your swords, men, let's go get him! I protected that man and his property, and he has repaid me evil for good."

Meanwhile, back at the ranch, a servant of Nabal's told Abigail that her husband had refused David's request. While her husband was a fool, Abigail was not. She knew that David would come to kill them all. She quickly gathered a lot of food, put it on the backs of donkeys, and headed out to try to stop the bloodshed.

So, we had two contingencies: one coming down the hill to seek war, and one riding up the hill to seek peace. When Abigail saw David, she got off her donkey and fell on her face. Rather than blaming her husband, she said, "Let the blame be mine. I did not see your men when they came. Please accept the food, and forgive me." What love! What courage! She did not wilt when the challenge came. She did not hide in a closet but faced the storm straight on.

David listened to her and then thanked her for stopping him from avenging himself. He took the food (he was a hungry man, after all!), and Abigail went back home. Within a few days, Nabal died. (I'm not sure anyone cried over it.) David, who was pretty sharp, recognized an amazing woman when he saw one. He heard about Nabal's death and asked Abigail to marry him.

So many times, when we encounter a storm, we are tempted to hide out. We might want to just stick our heads in the sand. If we do either, we will be swept away. Like Abigail, we must have the courage to face the storm.

ANCHOR 4: FOCUS

Even in the midst of the storm, we have to make decisions that produce the future we want. We can't lose sight of the shore. I read somewhere that if a twenty-one-year-old saved one hundred dollars a month, with compound interest he would have a million dollars by the time he was sixty. Sounds easy, but most of us can't do it—because something always comes along to make us lose focus. We want the million down the road, but today we want those new shoes or that DVD, so we don't save and we don't reach our goal. You and I cannot allow the storm we are in to cause us to lose sight of the shore. We must keep our focus.

The goal of Paul's trip was to ultimately get to Rome. Some of the sailors forgot that in the midst of the raging storm. They took their eyes off the target and looked at the waves. If Paul hadn't been on board making good decisions, all might have been lost.

Jesus visited His disciples one time by walking on the water. Peter thought that was pretty cool, so he asked Jesus if he could do it too. Jesus said, "Come on, Peter." Peter stepped out of the boat (that took courage!) and walked toward Jesus. He was doing fine until he took his eyes off Jesus and focused on the waves. Is it any easier to walk on the water when it is smooth than when it is full of waves? I don't think so!

In one of his teachings, my husband said that Vincent van Gogh could not afford paintbrushes, so he painted without them . . . because his focus was on his art.

Louis Pasteur continued to work on vaccines during the month that his three daughters died of the disease he was trying to prevent. He completed the vaccine the week after they died. His focus was on creating the vaccine, not the storm.

Michelangelo continued his work on the Sistine Chapel in spite of excruciating back pain. He forgot to eat, didn't get much sleep, and didn't change clothes. (I'm *not* saying this is good!) In fact, when he finally took his socks off, his skin came off with them. His focus was his work.

John Milton continued to write poetry while blind. Beethoven composed music even though deaf. Alexander the Great stormed back into battle with a deep wound in his side. The power of focus!

If we are going to make it through the storm, we have to remember our focus. If you are in a marital storm, you need to remember that your goal is to build a strong marriage. I have known many spouses who have faced serious storms. Some lost track of the target. Because the marriage was in a tough place, they began to shift their focus toward work. Rather than dropping anchors to weather the storm, they spent many hours at the office, because that didn't seem to be as painful. (It is not wrong to work hard at your career; it just shouldn't be a substitute for working on your marriage.) The more time they were away from their spouses, the more the marriages disintegrated. It wasn't long before the ship sank.

If you are in a financial storm, you can't lose focus. If you are going to make it to shore, you have to learn to live within a budget. Oh, that is very hard for me! I wasn't raised with the concept of a budget. If I wanted money, I just asked my dad for it. I know—I was a spoiled brat! When I married Philip, however, things changed. Sometimes he said I couldn't buy something because it wasn't in our budget. The first time he said that, I cried, because I thought we must be poor. "No," he assured me, "we have a budget so that we won't be poor." It still took me a while to get it . . . but eventually I did! If you are in a financial storm, stay focused on the budget, regardless of what you feel.

Sometimes we make decisions led by our emotions that can lead to a serious shipwreck. Emotions can work for us or against us. For example, our church has many wonderfully creative people. I love that! I love the actors, the dancers, the singers, the television producers—all of them. They have made our church fun, creative, and energetic. Like most of us, however, they could find their strength to be their weakness if they are not careful. It is their ability to tap into their emotions that helps them write amazing songs, feel the characters they portray, and dance with passion. But anyone who lets his emotions lead him discovers he is on his way to sinking.

We are to be grateful for our emotions but not be led by them. You can't pay your bills when you "feel" like it. No, you pay them when they are due. You can't just show up for work when you want. You go when you are expected to. You can't spend time with your kids or demonstrate your love for your husband only when it sounds like fun. You do those things regardless.

Weight loss is another emotional issue. So many women are in a health crisis because of their weight. I am not saying we all need to look like supermodels, but we do all need to be healthy. It is hard to fulfill our purpose on the earth if we are seriously overweight or underweight and unhealthy. Lots of us, because of storms in our health, have made the great decision to lose weight. But we have to be careful not to let our emotions get too involved. If we do, we will find ourselves eating ice cream and cake because we have had a hard day, rather than maintaining our focus on a healthy body.

> We are to be grateful for our emotions but not be led by them.

Sometimes we lose our focus because we have too much on our minds. Computer technicians say that running multiple programs at once is the cause of many technical problems. When we are in a storm, sometimes we try to do too many things, rather than the one thing we need to do to get to shore. We have many "good" alternatives . . . but most of the time, good is the enemy of the best.

Both my husband and my son have attention deficit disorder (ADD). This has certainly made our home an interesting one! Philip's challenge, when going through a storm, has always been keeping his focus. He will sit at his desk and start to work on something in an effort to handle the storm. Then he gets distracted and starts to work on something else . . . then something else . . . until his focus is diffused. I think a number of us that do this, whether we have ADD or not! (Maybe we have our own version of ADD: Amazingly Distracted Diva!)

Sometimes we lose our focus to temptation. I knew of a marriage one time that was in the midst of a storm. The wife became distracted by another man. She wasn't a bad person, she just stopped concentrating on strengthening her marriage—perhaps she lost hope, got tired of working on it. Understandable. Only now, her storm is even worse. Her loss of focus created an even bigger problem.

Sometimes we get distracted by things that are otherwise good. When I have faced storms in my marriage, I have been distracted not by another man, but by doing "good" things. Working on a marriage can be hard—exhausting, in fact; so rather than focusing on my relationship, I have decided to go and do "God's work." I will stay busy at church, preparing a message or writing. These are positive and necessary—but they are not excuses to ignore improving my marriage!

We can lose our focus because of a series of disappointments. Life is full of them, and some of us handle them better than others. Maybe you have faced various job rejections—certainly disappointing. You can respond in a number of ways. You can get angry and hate all employers. You can sit on the street corner and beg for money. Or you can keep applying for jobs, making an effort to become more hirable. Don't focus on the disappointment; look at where you want to go.

Whatever storm you are in, keep focused on the shore. Concentrate on destiny. Paul's destiny included going to Rome. He kept that in his mind. He focused on reaching his goal and not how bad the storm was.

Sometimes we have to quit obsessing over what we need and focus instead about what God has done for us so far. One day Jesus was talking with his disciples. They were a little panicked because they had traveled to the other side of the sea and had forgotten to bring bread. They wondered how they were going to eat. I can just see Jesus shaking His head as He asked, "Why are you worried about the bread? Don't you remember that we fed five thousand with just two loaves and five fish? Maybe you can tell Me how many leftovers there were."

I can just hear the disciples saying very quietly, "Ummm . . . twelve baskets full."

Jesus said, "I can't hear you . . . how many were there?"

Perhaps the disciples were a little embarrassed then, as they answered a little louder, "Twelve."

Jesus continued, "And if I'm not mistaken, we recently fed four thousand men with just seven loaves and a few fish. How many baskets were left over then?"

The disciples probably replied very sheepishly, "Seven."

Jesus asked, "What was that?"

The disciples replied a bit louder, "Seven large baskets of leftovers."

Was Jesus trying to embarrass them? No. He was sharpening their focus. Were they going to study the need before them and panic, or were they going to remember the provision He had made?

In the midst of the storm you are in, are you staring at the waves and the wind, or are you focusing on what He has done? He has seen you through all sorts of storms; He will see you through this one too. Quit talking about how bad your storm is. Don't compare your storm with someone else's ("You should see *my* storm! *My* waves are so big, you could surf them! *My* waves would sink an ocean liner"). Don't stare at the storm; focus on Him and His promises to you. Call someone on the phone, and rather than whining (yes, we all do this!), tell her a victory story from your past.

> He HAS SEEN YOU THROUGH ALL SORTS OF STORMS; He WILL SEE YOU THROUGH THIS one too.

LOOK BEYOND THE STORM

I decided to pursue a black belt in karate. On my journey to this goal, I had to break boards. (It's a great way to work off frustration—and much safer than breaking someone's head!) I learned that in order for me to split the board, I had to focus on a spot beyond the piece of wood . . . not on the board itself.

We set ourselves up for failure if we think only about what we are enduring. The writer of Hebrews challenged us to look away from all that will distract, and keep looking to Jesus, who is the leader and the source of our faith.

It takes everything in me not to let myself get distracted by the storm. But if I am going to reach the shore, I have to. Jesus was able to endure the storm of the Cross, not by dwelling on the nails and the betrayal, but by focusing on the joy before Him. He kept his mind on the fact that He would ultimately be sitting at the right hand of the Father; that once again, hurting human beings could have a loving relationship with their Creator: the victory, not the challenge. My husband says, "Losers focus on what they are going *through*. Champions focus on what they are going *to*."

> LOSERS FOCUS ON WHAT THEY ARE GOING *THROUGH*. CHAMPIONS FOCUS ON WHAT THEY ARE GOING *TO*.

Stay the course, my friend. Drop your anchors and hang on! Keep the shore in sight, maintaining courage to believe that you will reach it. You are the warrior chick, and His strength lives in you!!

God is within her, she will not fall; God will help her at break of day   Old Testament, Psalm Chapter 46, Verse 5 (NIV)

In times of difficulty,
you may feel
that your problems
will go on and on,
but they won't.
Every mountain has a top.
Every problem has a life span.
The question is,
who is going to give in first,
the frustration or you?
—Dr. Robert H. Schuller

SIX

DON'T ABANDON SHIP!

*Unless these men remain in the
ship, you cannot be saved.*

—New Testament,
Acts 27, verse 31

Where would we be if some of the amazing people in history quit their journeys simply because their seas got rough? I am in England now and am surrounded by thousands of years of history. As an American, I can be a little awestruck! Just today I was in the house of a woman who lived in the 1500s (very little closet space!). A plaque on the wall told her story. She was killed simply because she loved Jesus. She went to Mass and came home to be arrested . . . then tortured for what she believed. We owe much to some people in history who stayed their course and didn't abandon ship when it got rough.

Susan B. Anthony was ridiculed and persecuted simply because she thought every human being ought to be treated with dignity. She encountered armed threats and cruel crowds.

In 1856, the townspeople of Syracuse hanged her in effigy, then dragged her image through the streets. Still, in 1863, Susan helped to organize a Women's National Loyal League to support and petition for the Thirteenth Amendment, which would outlaw slavery—and it passed.

She then began to campaign for blacks' and women's full citizenship, including the right to vote, in the Fourteenth and Fifteenth Amendments. I am sure she was incredibly disappointed when the rights of women were not included in either of those amendments. But she didn't give up. A storm was raging all around her, and she didn't abandon ship. She persevered in spite of huge obstacles. I am sure at times she grew weary, but I am also sure that she knew that the goal—her shore—was always more important than her momentary discomfort.

Susan died in 1906. It wasn't until 1920 that women achieved the right to vote in the United States. She didn't get to see that dream reached. But somehow, I think she knows! Thank you, Susan Anthony, for not giving up. I, for one, am so grateful you didn't![1]

More Warrior Chicks from History

Harriet Tubman's life was not an easy one. She was born into slavery in 1820 and suffered greatly at the hands of her owners. In 1850, she escaped into Canada, but she didn't rest there. From 1851 until the end of the Civil War, she helped to rescue more than three hundred slaves and see them safely delivered to

Canada. Time and time again, she herself went back into the South, risking capture and certain death every time, because she wanted as many people freed as possible. Countless numbers owe their lives to Harriet Tubman. Thank you, Harriet, for not giving up![2]

Another heroine was only five when an illness left her partially blind, and then her mother died a few years later. After her father abandoned her, she lived in an orphanage. Obviously this young girl faced huge obstacles—her storm probably seemed unconquerable. But she didn't let the waves keep her down for long. She had a hunger to learn. A man visiting the orphanage heard of her insatiable passion for education, and her desire to go to school, so he arranged for her to go to Perkins Institution for the Blind in Boston. In spite of the difficulties, she loved it and gradually learned to read, using Braille.

She eventually graduated first in her class and underwent surgery that restored some of her sight. In 1887, she moved to Alabama to become the teacher and caretaker of a deaf-blind child. The child was Helen Keller, and the woman who persevered through all of the storms was Anne Sullivan. Through Anne's creativity, discipline, persistence, and patience, she was able to reach and then ultimately teach Helen. Against all odds, Helen eventually attended Radcliffe College and graduated with honors.

As Helen's teacher, Anne pioneered techniques of education for the handicapped and lobbied for increased opportunities for those without sight. Because of Anne's teaching success, Helen's life became an inspiration for many. Thank you, Anne, for not giving up, even though your life was full of overwhelming challenges.[3]

Stamina Makes the Man
(or the Chick!)

When the apostle Paul was awaiting his execution in prison, he wrote some pretty powerful words to his protégé, Timothy. In his final letter, he offered wisdom about the church, life, and the future. And he cast one last look over his shoulder, summarizing, "I have fought the good fight, I have finished the race, I have kept the faith."

Paul was a great man! Whole cities of people came to know God because of him, and he introduced the continent of Europe to the gospel. Paul wrote one half of the New Testament. His secret to greatness wasn't in his knowledge, though—and he was a knowledgeable guy. It wasn't in his looks. It wasn't because of his eloquence. Paul was extraordinary because he did not quit . . . no matter what!

> Everybody fails. Everybody takes his knocks, but the highly successful keep coming back. They stay in the game.
> —Sherry Lansing (as told to Walter Anderson)

After his conversion experience, Paul found the people around him hostile; they despised and mocked him. He could have said, "There is no love here. I'm throwing in the towel." But he didn't. Then the Christians didn't believe his conversion, and the Jews tried to kill him. He didn't quit. Paul was thrown into prison more than once. He didn't quit. He was involved in a shipwreck. He still didn't quit. He endured a cruel crowd's stoning him and leaving him for dead. How did he respond? He got up and returned to the city filled with the very people who wanted to kill him.

Just like the battery bunny, he kept going and going and going! Paul had plenty of opportunities to quit, plenty of exit roads off of destiny's path he could have taken. He didn't. There will be plenty of opportunities for us to quit too, lots of exits beckoning us off the path. We can't take them . . . no matter how hard the journey is . . . no matter how high the waves are!

Anybody ever felt like quitting? Sure. Most of us do at one point or another. And maybe there are a few things we should quit . . . our diet of doughnuts and fried everything, a ten-pack-a-day cigarette habit, a job that's going nowhere. But sometimes we give up things we need to keep working on: a marriage, a career, a weight-loss goal, an idea.

When Thomas Edison invented the lightbulb, he tried more than two thousand experiments before he got it to work. When asked how it felt to fail so many times, he said, "I never failed once. I invented the lightbulb. It just happened to be a two-thousand-step process."[4]

British fighter pilot Douglas Bader lost both legs in an air crash. He rejoined the British Royal Air Force, wearing two artificial limbs. During World War II, the Germans captured him three times, and three times, he escaped.[5]

In the 1940s, a young inventor named Chester Carlson took his idea to twenty corporations, including some of the biggest in the country. All rejected him. After seven long years of failure, he finally got the tiny Haloid Company in Rochester, New York, to purchase the rights to his electrostatic paper-copying process. Haloid became Xerox Corporation, and both it and Carlson became very rich.[6]

Henry Ford's first two companies failed. His third is doing very well!

During the 1968 Mexico City Olympics, one of the marathon runners was from Tanzania. He came into the arena headed for the finish line one hour after the winner had been announced. He came in bloodied, hurt and bandaged. A reporter asked the question, "Why didn't you quit?" The runner said, " My country did not send me to start the race, they sent me to finish it."

In 1915 Winston Churchill was forced to resign from public office. Everyone thought his political career was over—until twenty-five years later. In 1940, England turned to him because they "needed his bull dog determination to see them through their darkest hour."[7]

God has no problem using a sinner to further His purposes. He used Abraham, and Abraham was a liar. He used David, and David was an adulterer. He used Paul, and Paul was a murderer. After these three men repented, they didn't give up, and they became, respectively, the father of our faith; a king, psalmist, and lover of God; and the greatest apostle of the New Testament.

God doesn't have a problem using a failure either. When He called Moses, Moses was a broken-down shepherd stranded in the desert. Forty years earlier, he had tried to deliver Israel and failed. Gideon saw himself as an absolute zero. Peter denied that he knew the Lord . . . not once, but three times. God used them all. One gave the Law, one delivered the children of Israel from the Midianites, and one preached a sermon that changed more than three thousand lives. So, yes, God can and has used sinners and failures. What He can't use is a quitter.[8]

> ARISE [FROM THE DEPRESSION AND PROSTRATION IN WHICH CIRCUMSTANCES HAVE KEPT YOU—RISE TO A new LIFE]! SHINE!
> —OLD TESTAMENT, ISAIAH 60, VERSE 1

KEEP SWINGING

My husband is a huge baseball fan. In self-defense, I decided to become a fan as well. I have learned some of the players' names, the positions they play, and the rules of the game. I even yell like a maniac at the games. If I am going to be there, I might as well get into it!

Early in our marriage, Philip took me to my first professional baseball game. (I wasn't raised in the U.S., so my baseball education was sadly lacking!) At one point, Philip left to get us some hot dogs. Evidently, this is a part of the whole experience!

While he was gone, a batter hit a ball in our direction. People around me started screaming and standing up to try to catch the ball. I, on the other hand, ducked. I didn't want to get hit with a ball moving at a great speed, so I crouched down with my hands over my head. Well, the ball missed everyone's glove and hit the ground . . . right at my feet. And since I was looking down, I saw it. I picked it up, and all of the people around me moaned. I guess because I hadn't been trying to get the ball, it just wasn't fair that I did.

A few minutes later, Philip came back with our hot dogs and saw the ball in my hand. When I told him what had happened, he just shook his head. He laughed as he told me that he had been going to baseball games his whole life—with a glove—and had never caught a ball. And here it was my first game, and I had caught one! In the subsequent years, I have attended many games (no more balls, by the way!). Now I actually enjoy it.

In baseball, as you know, each batter has three strikes, and then he is out. But in real life, we can keep swinging and swinging until we get it right! I'm not out until I say I am out! So, regardless of the size of the storm, if I just keep going, I have a much better chance of reaching the shore. So don't quit on that marriage, don't quit on that business, don't quit on your family, don't quit on what God has asked you to do.

Please know that as you are going through your storm, you are surrounded by a "great cloud of witnesses." Know that as you weather your storm, all the hosts of heaven are cheering you on. You must make it through. You cannot let this storm sink you. A whole generation of people needs you to hand them the baton. They need the wisdom you will gain from getting through this storm.

> Know THAT AS YOU WEATHER YOUR STORM, ALL THE HOSTS OF HEAVEN ARE CHEERING YOU on.

I actually think it is very selfish of us to give up in the tough times. I know there are people we are supposed to help . . . just on the other side of this storm. Yes, life can knock us down, but you and I need to do whatever it takes to get ourselves back up. We owe it to the generations to come to keep going.

Others have to be our priority. On September 11, 2001, Flight 93 crashed in an isolated field in Pennsylvania. Having listened to some of what the passengers said on that flight, I am convinced that they, too, were willing to endure their storm for others. They made a decision in the midst of their storm that saved countless lives.

Jesus endured His storm (the Cross), the Bible tells us, "for the joy set before him." He didn't quit. He completed His journey because He saw us, you and me, in His future. We are the joy that was set before Him. He made it to His shore . . . for us.

Never Abandon Action

Good news about stormy seas: the longer I have walked with God, the shorter my recovery time has gotten. In years past, a storm could set me back for weeks, if not months. If a friend betrayed me, I could be down for a long time. If someone said something hurtful to me, I could stay hunched over for quite a while. But not anymore! I don't have that kind of time to waste. I cannot quit on what God has asked of me simply because of a storm. Too much is waiting for me on the shore!

One of the dictionary definitions of quitting is "to abandon necessary action." If I am going to get through rough waters, there are some actions I must not abandon. Athletes keep training through the pain. They won't get a medal otherwise.

John Eldredge told a story of a nineteenth-century Scottish discus thrower. He lived in the time before professional trainers and developed his skills alone in the highlands of Scotland. He made his own discus from a description he read in a book. What he didn't know was that the competition discus was made of wood with an outer rim of iron. His discus was made of pure metal, four times heavier than the ones used by his would-be challengers.

This committed Scotsman trained day after day, laboring under the burden of extra weight. He marked the record distance and kept working until he could throw his discus that far. He didn't quit, even though I'm sure becoming skillful took quite a bit of time and a lot of sore muscles.

Of course, at the competition, he threw the official wooden discus as if it were a puny tea saucer. He set new records, and for many years, none of his competitors could touch him. His persistence paid off.

Another definition of quitting is to simply give up—to admit defeat. Now, I may look defeated, I may feel defeated, but I am not going to admit defeat. Wanting to quit isn't bad. It is the actual quitting that will keep me from the shore I was destined to reach.

For Your Sake and Others', Stay with the Ship

When the pressure is on, most of us, like the sailors on Paul's journey, want to jump ship. We want to leave our marriages, our churches, our jobs. Sometimes a relationship or job or church is under construction. Maybe it feels like an earthquake! Please don't jump ship just because the seas are a little rough now. Do your part to make the relationship, job, or church strong again.

Paul told the guards on the ship, "If any man abandons the ship, all will be lost." Our decision to jump ship affects not only us, but all those around us. Recently, I have heard about quite a few couples in ministry who are getting divorced. I am not about to judge their hearts, but I am concerned about the

> OUR DECISION TO JUMP SHIP AFFECTS NOT ONLY US, BUT ALL THOSE AROUND US.

people who look to them for answers. I am sure thousands of church members around the world are confused and hurting simply because their leaders abandoned their marriages. The decisions we make at midnight . . . the roughest time . . . in the middle of a storm, will impact the lives of others. I really don't want to be responsible for messing up anyone else's life!

Stay with the ship. Keep acting for good; keep believing in the One who can calm the storm. Others are counting on you.

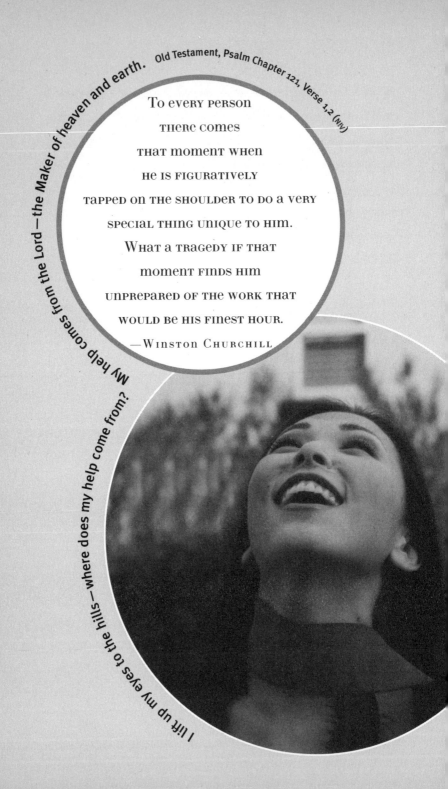

To every person there comes that moment when he is figuratively tapped on the shoulder to do a very special thing unique to him. What a tragedy if that moment finds him unprepared of the work that would be his finest hour.

—Winston Churchill

I lift up my eyes to the hills—where does my help come from? My help comes from the Lord—the Maker of heaven and earth. Old Testament, Psalm Chapter 121, Verse 1,2 (NIV)

seven

DO THE natuRaL STUFF

I beg you to eat something.
Your lives depend on it.

—New TesTamenT,
acTS 27, veRSe 34 (cev)

I can't imagine being so stressed that I couldn't eat. It is hard to believe that Paul had to remind the men on his ship to have dinner. But I have found that when we are in a storm, sometimes we forget to do the normal things that need doing.

I knew a woman who was on a serious diet. She had to lose more than one hundred pounds—no easy feat. She was doing quite well, when suddenly some stuff came up at work that stressed her out. She was in a workplace storm. People were being moved around within the office, no one was sure he would have a job the next day. Her job description changed regularly. It's understandable that she felt a bit tossed about.

But she started saying things like, "Oh, there is too much

going on right now. I'm too upset. I think I'll have that piece of pizza." She gave up her diet, gained back the previously lost pounds (plus some more), and felt more discouraged than ever.

Another woman faced a storm in her marriage. She and her husband seemed to be drifting apart, and she was scared. He was working more and more hours; they couldn't seem to find time to connect. She just about stopped eating. Her energy level dropped, her temper sharpened, and she was even less able to give in the marriage.

Another woman was dealing with her teenage son. (God help all of us who are!!) He was pushing every limit (must be the job description!). His grades were not great. He didn't seem interested in church. She found some pornography on his computer. A teenage storm. She was so worried about him that she couldn't give time or attention to the rest of her family. She wasn't interested in sex or dates with her husband—she was too focused on the storm raging in her son.

A friend's betrayal can be one of the worst things we face. Susan was suffering. Her heart was broken. She had given so much to this friendship, and now it seemed beyond repair. Her friend not only lied about her but tried to sabotage her business. She knew she must begin the process of forgiveness, but at the moment, she just wanted to scream. Friend storm. At work she wasn't doing her job; she was snapping at innocent people and falling seriously behind.

Kathy had just lost her father. Death is always a very rough storm. She and her father hadn't been close, but now they wouldn't ever get that opportunity. Her sadness affected every area of her life. She just wanted to sit on the sofa in the dark. She lapsed beyond grief into depression.

I knew a single mom who had been very ready for a boyfriend. Understandable. She began a relationship, however, more from desperation than wisdom. The relationship did not last long, and she was heartbroken. Relationship storm. She cried, moped around, stayed home from work, got angry with her friends . . . and basically forgot that she had a child who needed her love and help, regardless of her love life.

All of these storms are serious, and I am aware that they are very painful. I would just like to suggest that if we are going to make it out of them, we can't let the storm itself eclipse our everyday, normal lives.

Everybody fails. Everybody takes
his knocks, but the highly
successful keep coming back.
They stay in the game.
—Sherry Lansing (as told to Walter Anderson)

Life Versus Storm

One time in our church, we were confronting some very serious people issues. A storm was brewing. We spent hours trying to help someone make the right decision. It was exhausting, and I always left the office drained. My friend Michelle knew what I was dealing with at work, and because she was doing some work for me at home, she saw me come in every evening. I changed clothes and then started doing homework with my daughter, I took my son to the gym, or I started dinner. To me, those are everyday, normal occurrences. Michelle paid me a compliment, though she didn't know it. She said, "I am amazed that you can leave the heart-wrenching stuff that you were dealing with at work, and then just come in here as if there was nothing going on."

It didn't occur to me to do otherwise. Yes, there was a storm at work, but I still had to take care of the other aspects of life. My children needed my attention—they needed me to cheer from the bleachers at their games or drive them different places. My husband needed his wife—her love, affection, and time. Life goes on, regardless of how big the waves are. (Just so you know . . . I haven't always been able to do this! It has been a process. There were plenty of times previously, and you'll read about some later, where I let a storm dominate every aspect of my life.)

Paul reminded the Corinthian church that the natural came first, then the spiritual. God created the heavens and the earth . . . the spiritual and the natural. Sometimes, as Christians, we focus too much on the spiritual and disregard the natural. I don't want to be known as someone who is so spiritually minded that I'm no earthly good! The Scriptures are filled with powerful spiritual dynamics, but at the same time, they show us the wisdom of God in practical steps that we can follow. Spiritual is not the opposite of natural. Practical is not the opposite of powerful. Practical is the pathway to the powerful. James said, "I will show you my faith by what I do." In other words, "I'll show you my faith in the natural steps I take."

We shouldn't be great at the prayer meeting and lousy at paying our bills. We shouldn't be passionate when worshiping God and horrible at showing up on time. Let's be terrific at both! So many times we try to show our faith by being mystical, super-spiritual, yet basically we do nothing . . . hoping God will step in and rescue us.

> We DO OUR PART SO THAT GOD can DO HIS PART.

Right now, in the midst of our storm, it's time for us to act. We do our part so that God can do His part. If you are in a financial storm, you can't just sit in your living room and pray. Certainly, pray first—but then you have to *do.* You go out looking for a job; He can open the door for you. You do the natural things—give offerings, live by a budget, and work hard. You sow the financial seed, and He brings the financial harvest. We can't just sit around and wait for God to rescue us. In Chapter 8, I will talk about the importance of looking to God, but in this chapter, I am challenging us to do what we can to get us to shore.

Some everyday activities we need to make sure we're doing, even in the midst of a ferocious storm!

ESSENTIAL STORM ACTIVITIES

KEEP THOSE MUSCLES MOVING

One of the biggest dangers of a storm is that we can get weary, then depressed. I am not making light of depression. I know plenty of people who are on antidepressants. But sometimes I wonder if their depression came and remained because they forgot to do the normal stuff when they encountered storms.

Physical activity is crucial if we are going to stay healthy for a lifetime, and it is very important that we don't neglect it during a storm. Researchers at Duke, Harvard, and Stanford Universities have shown repeatedly that exercise is powerful medicine for both anxiety (which is what we generally feel during a storm!) and depression (another common side effect). The Duke team found that adults with major depression who worked out every day (a half hour of aerobics, fifteen minutes each of warm-up and cooldown) did just as well after four months as a group taking Zoloft. In a six-month follow-up, the exercisers were more likely to be partially or fully recovered than those on medication, and less likely to relapse: 8 percent versus 38 percent.[1]

> REGULAR EXERCISE WILL GO A LONG WAY TOWARD SEEING YOU TO SHORE.

I am not telling you to go off of any medication. I am simply suggesting that in the midst of the hard times, don't forget to keep your body strong. Regular exercise will go a long way toward seeing you to shore. The truth is, I never feel like exercising, even when no storm is raging. I don't like exercise. I do it anyway.

Life is not going to get easier, or any less busy. That is a fact—unless you totally withdraw from society and become a recluse. We are supposed to be touching our world, not running from it! By being a part of the world and by loving people, we will encounter storms regularly. We have got to become great riders of the storm!

I go to the gym and work out, not because I am trying to win a bodybuilding contest (God knows . . . that will never happen!), but because I am trying to build some muscles, keep my heart healthy, and limit the fat percentage on my body to a reasonable level. I have scoliosis and can often experience pain in my back. I have found, however, that if I strengthen my abdominal muscles, my back is stronger and hurts less. Do you know how I strengthen my abs? By doing hundreds of different kinds of stomach crunches, leg lifts, and sit-ups. Is doing them ever fun? *No!!* But I do them anyway, because I know I need to be strong to accomplish all that I am put here to do.

Also, by physically taking care of my body, I have found that I just feel better. And when I feel good, I make better decisions than when I am physically weak. When I am physically weak, the storms seem so huge and the shore so far away. We have big lives to live and some serious storms to endure, so let's get strong! I don't care if you are eighteen or seventy-eight: you can start now to do something physically that will help you weather the storm.

TAKE A NAP!

In the midst of a crisis, it is easy to work so hard that we forget to rest. But if we are going to reach the shore, we must!

I knew someone who sat at her very sick child's bedside hour after hour. Of course, we all want to be with our children in their hours of need, but we cannot do this at the expense of our own health. That just creates another storm. That is what happened in this situation. The mom got sick, because she didn't take time to rest.

I knew someone else who was going through a storm at work. She did get days off, but on those days, she did not do things that replenished her soul. So when she went back to work, she was just as worn out as when she left. Rest should involve not only replenishing the body, but the soul.

God worked hard for six days, and then He rested. What is restful for you? Find out what that is. It might include reading, going for a walk, coffee with a friend, sleeping, praying, worshiping, a movie, dinner out . . . whatever. Just make sure you are taking a few moments of rest—physically, emotionally, mentally, and spiritually—in the midst of your storm.

EAT GOOD STUFF (AT LEAST MOST OF THE TIME!)

As I mentioned, it is hard for me to imagine that Paul had to remind the men on his ship to eat. But I have encountered some women, who, when under pressure, stop eating. Their energy drops, their tempers soar, and their health weakens. They don't have the strength to make it to shore. And remember: reaching the shore is not optional. We must!

One time Saul's army and his son, Jonathan, were battling the Philistines. The army had been fighting for days without eating. Jonathan found some honey in the woods and ate it. When he did, his weariness left, and "his eyes brightened."

He told the others they would have been better off eating some of their plunder than passing food by—it would have strengthened them.

> Don't reach for pizza and ice cream just because you are feeling the stress.

Paul told the Galatians not to grow weary in acting nobly or doing right. He said that they would reap if they just kept sowing. Sometimes exhaustion claims us because we are just not eating right. We are not providing the fuel that our bodies need.

Starving ourselves doesn't help anything. It will merely create another storm. So, please, remember to eat in the middle of the storm. And remember to eat well. A diet of fast food will not produce the results you want. It may be quick, but it is not the best for you.

If you are overweight and have changed your eating patterns in a healthier way, good for you! But don't get off course when a storm enters your life. Don't reach for pizza and ice cream just because you are feeling the stress. Maintain the healthy habits you established before the storm began to rage. Eating, and eating healthily, provides the natural fuel we need to overcome mighty waves and high winds.

STAY CONNECTED WITH FRIENDS AND WORKPLACE

Managing to continue to do a good job at work is crucial, no matter how big the storm might be. I have known people who just up and quit their jobs because they had a relationship meltdown. Or they began to perform so badly, they were fired. Not good. Then they just had another storm to weather!

My friend Noriko is amazing in quite a few ways. She can accomplish in one day what would take most people a week to do. She has overcome a very challenging childhood and manages to smile at some point every day!

In the last few years, I have seen her face a horrible storm. Noriko's daughter, Brittany, was diagnosed with leukemia when she was eight. The severe kind. The adult kind. (I didn't know there were different degrees of leukemia, but there are.) I'm not sure I can imagine a more devastating storm for a mom. It is one thing for adults to be in pain, but when our children suffer . . . well, there just are no words.

During Brittany's first few months of treatment, Noriko basically isolated herself. For many years she had been handling problems on her own, so she continued to do so. She did not want to need people, so she didn't invite anyone in to help shoulder the burden. She ate junk food, because it was easier. She quit working out. She avoided friends, work, and the church. She pulled up the anchors rather than dropping them.

Every aspect of her life suffered because she forgot to do the natural stuff during the storm. Still, the doctors did eventually get the leukemia into remission, and we all rejoiced!

Within a few years, the leukemia came back with a vengeance. This time Brittany's chances of survival were even slimmer. She needed a bone marrow transplant. We had no idea how hard this would be. Noriko learned that because Brittany is a combination of different races, finding a bone marrow donor would be an extra-hard challenge. But they did find a donor—one. Thank God! In all of their data bank, they had only one who was a perfect match.

In preparation for the transplant, Brittany had to undergo chemotherapy. This time Noriko handled the storm very differently. She reached out to people. She kept up with her friends. She did her best not to let the hospital dominate her life.

The battle for Brittany's health is not over yet, and I continue to marvel at my friend. She is at the hospital when she needs to be, and yet she is not neglecting her friendships, her husband, or her son. She is watching what she eats, knowing it will affect her strength for other tasks. She is finding time to exercise. She is working, when she can fit it in around her daughter's treatment schedule. Noriko refuses to let the storm set the parameters of her whole life, though in this instance it would certainly be easy to do.

CORRAL THOSE WILD EMOTIONS

One of our greatest challenges during a storm is managing our emotions. I just watched the movie *What About Bob?* Richard

Dreyfuss played a psychiatrist whose former patient stalked him. The patient, played by Bill Murray, was basically a harmless, hurting guy. He showed up in New Hampshire, where Richard and his family were on vacation. Everyone else liked and befriended Bill, but Richard just wanted him to go away. He tried all sorts of ploys to get him out of his house. Nothing worked.

Richard started to lose it. He began to act irrationally. In his frustration, he decided to blow up Bill with dynamite. Through a series of events, he actually ended up blowing up his own home. It was sort of funny, in a sick way! The truth is, Richard had brought disaster on himself, because he couldn't control his emotions at a crucial time.

I remember a time when I came home from a rather challenging day. I had had a conflict at work and a tough situation with a friend. As I picked up my son from school, he said something with just enough disrespect that it set me off! Yes, he needed to be corrected, but I went way over the top. I reacted because of a storm I was facing in another area of my life, rather than responding appropriately to this specific situation.

Emotions are an incredible gift, yet most of the time I find that rather than our managing them, they control us. We do so many things because we "feel" or "don't feel" like it. And as I've said in other places throughout the book, this can get us in serious trouble and will certainly prolong any storm.

I think recognizing that our emotions can lead us down a

destructive path will go a long way toward not allowing them to do so. And just take a breath . . . don't say every word that your emotions are driving you to.

REMEMBER YOU ARE A WIFE AND MOTHER (IF YOU ARE!)

I know of a couple in Australia who recently went through a storm in their marriage. The truth is that they both stopped trying, so the marriage seemed boring and mundane. And when Miss Cute and Exciting walked by in her bikini . . . he followed. A divorce quickly ensued.

The storm continues to rage. This couple had children in their thirties—not young, certainly, but still needing Mom and Dad. Both parents, in their quests for new and exciting lives, were too occupied with their own happiness to be parents. They were busy trying to find new partners.

In the storm, they forgot to continue showing love and giving time to their children. One of the kids is planning her wedding for next year and now wonders if she even wants her parents to attend. I think she will come around, but still, the whole thing was unnecessary. If the couple, while in the midst of their storm, had remembered they were parents, there would still have been at least partial health in this family.

Truly, storms will come and go in our

> PLEASE DON'T LET YOUR MARRIAGE BECOME ANOTHER STORM SIMPLY BECAUSE YOU NEGLECTED IT.

lives . . . and I want to weather them with my husband and kids. I want Philip to be a constant in my life, so I can't let other pressures overshadow my relationship with him. This is true whether we are dealing with storms at work, with the children, with friends, or with finances. Please don't let your marriage become another storm simply because you neglected it. Marriages don't survive being placed on the back burner.

A young couple I knew in college wrestled with some issues in their new marriage. She was attending medical school, taking a full load of classes—and was struggling with some of them—as well as working part time. He was also working part time. She wanted her new husband to let her focus just on school until she graduated, and then she would devote herself to the marriage.

Now, I can certainly understand wanting to do great at medical school—but not at the expense of a marriage. As her friend, I challenged her about this mind-set and warned that if she didn't contribute to the marriage, she wouldn't have one in a few years. Sadly, the relationship collapsed, and I think it is because in the midst of the challenges, they did not do the natural building that every couple has to do.

Keep a Storm in Its Place

We have to work hard at not letting the storm be our whole lives. If we do, the storm will *take over*.

If you are married, help each other out with this. I have said to Philip, "Yes, that is a horrible thing going on. It could be scary for us as a church if we don't get that property. But we—you and I—are okay, our children are healthy, we have a vacation coming up, the church is growing by leaps and bounds," etc. And he has said to me, "I'm sorry that person hurt your feelings. She shouldn't have betrayed you like that. Here's a tissue, and remember: we are okay, the children got good grades this quarter, Christmas is coming, and forty people got saved last weekend at church." It is easy to let the storm in one area totally eclipse every other area of life. Try hard not to let it!

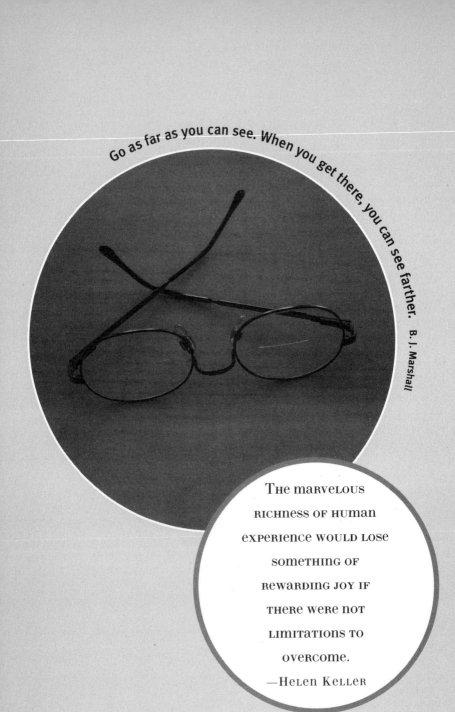

Go as far as you can see. When you get there, you can see farther. —B.J. Marshall

THE MARVELOUS RICHNESS OF HUMAN EXPERIENCE WOULD LOSE SOMETHING OF REWARDING JOY IF THERE WERE NOT LIMITATIONS TO OVERCOME.

—HELEN KELLER

eIGHT

Remember who is on the throne

Giving thanks to God . . .

—New Testament,
ACTS 27, VERSE 35

I love this story.

According to John Gipson, it happened in Galveston, Texas. It concerned a woman and her parakeet named "Chippie." It seems that the woman was cleaning Chippie's birdcage with a canister vacuum cleaner. She was cleaning the bottom of the cage with no attachment on the tube, when the telephone rang. She turned her head to pick up the phone, continuing to vacuum the cage and as she said, "hello" into the phone, she heard the horrible sound of Chippie being sucked up into the vacuum. Immediately she put down the phone, ripped open the vacuum bag, and found Chippie in there, stunned but still alive.

Since the bird was covered with dust and soot, she grabbed it, ran into the bathroom, turned on the faucet, and held the bird under the water to clean it off. When she finished that, she saw the hair dryer on the bathroom sink. She turned it on and held the bird in front of the blast of hot air to dry him off.

A few weeks later a reporter from the newspaper that originally published the story went out to the house to ask the woman, "How's Chippie doing now?" She said, "Well, Chippie doesn't sing much any more. He just sort of sits and stares."

Many of us can identify with Chippie at some point. Life has sucked us up, thrown cold water on us, and blown us away. And somewhere in the trauma we have lost our song."[1]

If we are not only going to make it through the storms, but arrive at the shore stronger, we *must* remember that our God will never abandon us. We must remember that He holds us in His hands.

The Strength of Eagles

I love the words that the prophet Isaiah used:

Surely you know.
  Surely you have heard.
The LORD is the God who lives forever,
  who created all the world.
He does not become tired or need to rest.
  No one can understand how great his wisdom is.
He gives strength to those who are tired
  and more power to those who are weak.
Even young children become tired and need to rest,
  and young people trip and fall.

But the people who trust the LORD will become strong again.

They will rise up as an eagle in the sky;

> they will run and not need rest;

> they will walk and not become tired. (This is my dream!!)

(Isaiah 40:28–31 NCV)

My husband has enjoyed learning about eagles over the years. When we first got married, he collected not only eagle stories, but figurines of the majestic creatures. Needless to say, in the earthquake, all of the lovely crystal, china, and ceramic eagles became dust! If anyone knows where I can get a Tupperware eagle . . . just let me know!

Philip tells me that a certain type of eagle can, at one stage in his life, develop a wartlike growth on his beak. This eagle's life begins to change. Normally, a healthy eagle can spot his prey from two miles away and swoop down on it with amazing precision at one hundred miles per hour. But now, the eagle dives for prey and misses. He slowly loses his accurate sense of perception and some cannot hunt effectively. He grows weary, loses his strength. When he lands, his balance is off, and he stumbles to a stop.

With the diminishing of his skills, he seems to get confused and doubt his own abilities. The eagle actually begins to appear depressed, and soon he starts to lose his beautiful feathers. He retreats to the darkness of a cave, continuing to weaken.

Then something interesting happens. It is as though the eagle plans suicide. Either he wants to destroy himself, or he realizes that he is about to die; he decides he might as well do some flying. Perhaps he remembers what it was to soar above the clouds, to be the king of the air. He steps out of the cave, looks toward heaven, and begins to flap his tired wings. He lifts off and heads straight up. He goes higher and higher toward the heavens. He rises above the clouds and keeps on going.

As he continues to gain altitude, and as he goes through the atmosphere pressure changes, the growth on his beak bursts. When it bursts, he is immediately energized with fresh power and strength.

His equilibrium returns. His depth perception comes back. He is once again himself. He can hunt with precision and strengthen himself.

Isaiah told us that if we would trust God and remember that He is on the throne, then we, too, would rise like the eagle. In the midst of the storm, keep looking up. It is easy to get freaked out—or at least, distracted by the waves—but never forget Who is taking care of you. Don't let the challenge you are facing cause you to hide yourself in a cave!

Savvy Strategy for a Storm

Storms challenge our belief systems. When the waves are crashing against us, we find out where our trust is. I recently heard a pastor in Australia, Tim Edwards, tell of a day when he, his younger brother, and his brother-in-law went ocean fishing. A severe storm came up, and the boat couldn't withstand the waves. Eventually it sank. Tim's brother and brother-in-law were killed, and Tim found himself alone in the middle of raging water. I can't imagine feeling more isolated.

WHEN THE WAVES ARE CRASHING AGAINST US, WE FIND OUT WHERE OUR TRUST IS.

His brother and brother-in-law had been believers, so Tim knew he would see them again in heaven, but I'm not sure how much comfort that was as he tried to keep his head above water. Tim described wanting to quit so many times. He was so tired of swimming toward shore, he thought it would be easier to just let himself sink. But every time he tried to stop, he couldn't. He sensed the presence of God urging him on.

Eventually he reached a buoy and hung on, singing Darlene Zschech's song, "Shout to the Lord." After watching his boat sink, seeing his family die, spending nineteen hours in the sea while singing praise to God, Tim was rescued. Whew! I'm sure it was with bittersweet relief that he reached safety. I can't help thinking it was his worshiping and crying out to God that saved him and sustained him through the heartache of losing his brother and brother-in-law.

LOOKING FOR STRENGTH IN ALL THE RIGHT PLACES

While David and his mighty men were away from their home, an enemy came in and burned the town, then kidnapped their wives and children. What a horrible thing to have happened.

David and his men came home after battle only to find they had no home. Those they loved were gone. A definite storm. What was David's response to this crisis?

The first thing he did was cry! (I feel better already!) It is okay to cry . . . to be real. In fact, the book of 1 Samuel tells us that David and his men cried until they were too weak to cry any more. That is some serious weeping. But that isn't all they did. When he finished grieving, David strengthened himself in God. He remembered Who was on the throne. I'm sure some of the men wanted to stay in grief, some wanted to stone David, and some wanted immediately to go fight. But David knew that he needed God's reinforcement before he did anything else.

Strengthening yourself in God does require some work! I heard a story of a new infantryman who asked his commanding officer, "Sir, where is my foxhole?" The officer's quick reply was "You're standing on it—just throw the dirt out!"

It is the same for you and me. The strength of God is near; we just have to do a little work to get it. Have you read the Bible lately? Not just reflected on how important Scripture is, but actually read God's Word? Have you taken time to worship God?

Some say, "I know how important worship is." But what I'm asking is, *Have you worshiped Him?* Worship has nothing to do with singing in key (which is a good thing, since I can't!). It isn't even necessarily singing. It is declaring Who He is. He is our God . . . our Protector . . . our Comforter . . . our Healer . . . our

Peace . . . our Provider. My friend Darlene Zschech says that worship includes words from a heart that is yearning for more of God and less of oneself. This holds the key to many victories and delights the heart of our Father. When we worship God, we can see our problem from His perspective. Our huge storm suddenly looks manageable!

GOD IN THE MIDST

David told God, "The praises of Israel are your throne." He inhabits our worship! And I know there is not one situation that God's presence can't make better.

Acts 16 tells us that Roman soldiers beat Paul and Silas because of their faith. They flogged the men to within an inch of their lives. Bleeding and in serious pain, Paul and Silas found themselves in prison. Somehow, in this horror, they began to praise God. They began to sing to Him.

PRISONERS, HURTING PEOPLE, ARE ALL AROUND US, WATCHING, LISTENING, AND NEEDING WHAT WE HAVE. KEEP THAT IN MIND!

I don't think this was a conscious plan. I don't think Paul said to Silas, "Look, let's sing and praise God, and then He'll send an earthquake to deliver us." No. I imagine that in a cracked, hurting voice, Paul asked, "Silas, how are you doing?" I can hear Silas just moan, and then maybe Paul said, "You know, Silas, the only thing that will improve this place is His presence. We need the presence of God."

They reminded themselves Who was on the throne. And, as they praised Him, He entered the scene. He always does.

As a side note: it says the other prisoners were listening to Paul and Silas's giving praise. I'm sure those men were also in pain, but by the end, they probably wanted what Paul and Silas had. We know the jailer did. I think it is the same in our lives. Prisoners, hurting people, are all around us, watching, listening, and needing what we have. Keep that in mind!

> [GOD] WILL YET FILL YOUR MOUTH WITH LAUGHTER AND YOUR LIPS WITH SHOUTS OF JOY.
> —OLD TESTAMENT, JOB 8, VERSE 21 (NIV)

WHAT (OR WHO) HAS YOUR TRUST

Mark tells the story of when Jesus and the disciples crossed the sea. Jesus had just spent the day with lots of people...teaching them and giving them principles to live by. I'm sure He was ready for a rest. At the end of the day, He told the disciples that they should all get into the boat and cross to the other side of the sea. He got into the boat too, and immediately went to sleep. As they were crossing, a huge storm of hurricane proportions arose. The word that is translated as "arose" literally means . . . "unexpected or taken by surprise." Of course the disciples were taken by surprise by the storm; they were fishermen. They knew what the sky and water looked like before a storm. They never would have left the shore if they thought a storm was coming.

So, yes they were surprised to find the waves beating against their boat. They were freaking out!

We read that they woke Jesus up. (No faith involved . . . they just wanted him awake as they all drowned!) And the word "awoke" in this story is the same word that is used to mean "resurrection."[2] That is a pretty powerful awakening!! They jerked him up and said, "Hey man, don't you care about us?? We are perishing!!" Jesus barely had time to wipe the sleep out of his eyes before he took care of the situation. He rebuked the wind and the waves. He said, "Be still . . . muzzled!" And the wind ceased—sank to rest as if exhausted by its beating—and there was immediately a great calm, a perfect peacefulness.[3] Then He turned to His buddies, His disciples, and challenged them about their lack of faith. Basically He was saying, "Don't you know that you could have done this too?" He was dropping the same authority on them. He has given it to us. We have the ability to calm the storms in our life, simply (actually there is nothing simple about it!) by faith.

Mark 6 tells us of the miraculous feeding of the five thousand. Right after that amazing occurrence, Jesus again sent the boys to the other side of the lake. (Another boat—another day!) He was taking some time alone to pray, and He wanted them to go ahead of Him. So the disciples got in their boat and began to row, just as Jesus instructed. Then a big storm came up. I heard Pastor Danny Chambers say that sometimes we face the greatest storms in the middle of obedience.

Jesus wasn't with the men when choppy waters and gusts of

wind hit, and I wonder if the disciples said things like "Hey, He sent us here! Why couldn't He have warned us?" The disciples strained at the oars. It's hard work, rowing in a storm (actually, it's hard work rowing anytime!), and I imagine they wished they were back at the miracle service, feeding the thousands. That was fun. Having loaves of bread multiplying in your hands: man, that was cool! This sweating while rowing in a storm definitely wasn't!

Like many of us in a midnight storm, they were probably wondering where Jesus was.

Then they saw Jesus, walking toward them on the water. Actually they were so freaked out, they thought He was a ghost! But as He got closer, they recognized Him. I'm sure they were relieved. *Whew! Jesus is here!* But the Bible tells us that Jesus would have walked past them. Can you believe it? There were His friends, struggling in the boat, and He would have walked past them. I am sure they were shocked as Jesus started to stroll by. But in one way it makes sense. He had told them to go to the other side. He must have thought they had the ability to do it—storms and all.

It was the same when Jesus told Peter at the Last Supper that the devil had asked to sift him like wheat. I'm sure Peter thought that Jesus would have told the devil, "No way!" Instead, He said to the disciple, "I prayed that your faith would see you through." I doubt this is what Peter had in mind.

Like most of us in the middle of our storm, the disciples thought that their need was the greatest. But what if someone else had a greater need on the shore where Jesus was headed? Maybe this is too weird of a thought. But I think sometimes we forget that our Father is on the throne, and that He has given us the ability to get through some storms. We always think that our need is the greatest, and that we can't possibly get through it.

I heard Danny Chambers say another time that our greatest temptation in a storm is to put our trust in something other than God. Rather than losing our heads and thinking we just need another joint, drink, or man to see us through, let's remember Who is on the throne. He thinks we can get through this! If I have the faith that I am going to heaven, surely I have the faith to endure some wind and waves!

We Got Grace

Mary and Martha were grieving because their brother, Lazarus, was dead. When they finally saw Jesus, their despair did not lessen. They should have known better. They knew Jesus. Don't we?

The apostle Paul told the Corinthian church that he suffered from a "thorn in my flesh." Sounds painful. He knew it was from the enemy, and he wanted God to take it away. He wanted out of the storm. Fair enough. Most of us do. But that is not what God did for Paul. God told him, "My grace is enough for you. It is sufficient against any danger and enables you to bear the trouble manfully (or in my case, womanfully!). We have been given the grace to go through the storm.

Oftentimes, when I have reached my end—when I have done all I know to do—that is when He makes Himself strong! My job is to put on the armor that Paul described to the Ephesians: truth, integrity, stability, faith, and salvation. Then I am supposed to stand . . . knowing that He is on the throne.

Pastor Jentezen Franklin said that when a storm hits, God can do one of two things: calm the storm, or calm me in the midst of it. He is in charge. Never forget that!

God's Deliverance

Lisa Beamer reflected on the loss of her dad in her book, *Let's Roll.*

> Slowly I began to understand that the plans God has for us don't just include "good things," but the whole array of human events. The "prospering" He talks about in the book of Jeremiah is often the outcome of a "bad" event. I remember my mom saying that many people look for miracles—things that in their human minds "fix" a difficult situation. Many miracles, however, are not a change to the normal course of human events; they are found in God's ability and desire to sustain and nurture people through even the worst situations. Somewhere along the way, I stopped demanding that God fix the problems in my life and started to be thankful for His presence as I endured them.[4]

Over and over, Scripture reminds us: regardless of the storm we find ourselves in, our God can get us through it!

Oh thank GOD—he's so good!

    His love never runs out.

All of you set free by GOD, tell the world!

    Tell how he freed you from oppression,

Then rounded you up from all over the place,

    from the four winds, from the seven seas.

Some of you wandered for years in the desert,

    looking but not finding a good place to live,

Half-starved and parched with thirst,

    staggering and stumbling, on the brink of exhaustion.

Then, in your desperate condition, you called out to GOD.

    He got you out in the nick of time;

He put your feet on a wonderful road

    that took you straight to a good place to live.

So thank GOD for his marvelous love,

    for his miracle mercy to the children he loves.

He poured great draughts of water down parched throats;

    the starved and hungry got plenty to eat.

Some of you were locked in a dark cell,

    cruelly confined behind bars,

Punished for defying God's Word,

    for turning your back on the High God's counsel—

A hard sentence, and your hearts so heavy,

    and not a soul in sight to help.

Then you called out to GOD in your desperate condition;

    he got you out in the nick of time.

He led you out of your dark, dark cell,
    broke open the jail and led you out.
So thank GOD for his marvelous love,
    for his miracle mercy to the children he loves;
He shattered the heavy jailhouse doors,
    he snapped the prison bars like matchsticks!
Some of you were sick because you'd lived a bad life,
    your bodies feeling the effects of your sin;
You couldn't stand the sight of food,
    so miserable you thought you'd be better off dead.
Then you called out to GOD in your desperate condition;
    he got you out in the nick of time.
He spoke the word that healed you,
    that pulled you back from the brink of death.
So thank GOD for his marvelous love,
    for his miracle mercy to the children he loves;
Offer thanksgiving sacrifices,
    tell the world what he's done—sing it out!

Some of you set sail in big ships;
    you put to sea to do business in faraway ports.
Out at sea you saw GOD in action,
    saw his breathtaking ways with the ocean:
With a word he called up the wind—
    an ocean storm, towering waves!
You shot high in the sky, then the bottom dropped out;
    your hearts were stuck in your throats.

You were spun like a top, you reeled like a drunk,
  you didn't know which end was up.
Then you called out to GOD in your desperate condition;
  he got you out in the nick of time.
He quieted the wind down to a whisper,
  put a muzzle on all the big waves.
And you were so glad when the storm died down,
  and he led you safely back to harbor.
So thank GOD for his marvelous love,
  for his miracle mercy to the children he loves.
Lift high your praises when the people assemble,
  shout Hallelujah when the elders meet!

GOD turned rivers into wasteland,
  springs of water into sunbaked mud;
Luscious orchards became alkali flats
  because of the evil of the people who lived there.
Then he changed wasteland into fresh pools of water,
  arid earth into springs of water,
Brought in the hungry and settled them there;
  they moved in—what a great place to live!
They sowed the fields, they planted vineyards,
  they reaped a bountiful harvest.
He blessed them and they prospered greatly;
  their herds of cattle never decreased.
But abuse and evil and trouble declined
  as he heaped scorn on princes and sent them away.

He gave the poor a safe place to live,
>   treated their clans like well-cared-for sheep.
Good people see this and are glad;
>   bad people are speechless, stopped in their tracks.
If you are really wise, you'll think this over—
>   *it's time you appreciated GOD's deep love.*
(Psalm 107, THE MESSAGE, italics mine)

I know this is a huge portion of Scripture, but I just love the picture the whole thing presents. Regardless of the storm we find ourselves in, our God can get us through it!

Some people found themselves in a desert: hungry, thirsty, no place to call home. But then God stepped in, satisfied the hunger and thirst, and led them home.

Some found themselves in a prison of depression and emotional suffering. Then He saved them; He brought them out of their gloom and darkness.

ARE YOU ALL ALONE? REMEMBER WHO IS ON THE THRONE!

Some even turned away from God, were in misery and alone. But His love healed them, and they were saved.

Some were in a stormy sea, the waves crashing around them. They lost their courage. They did not know what to do. But then He calmed the storm, stilled the waves, and guided them to port.

I don't know what kind of storm you are in at the moment. If it is the barren, dry desert kind, He will satisfy your thirst.

Maybe you feel hopeless in your marriage. Perhaps you are choking in the chains of depression. Maybe your financial situation is desperate. Are you all alone? Remember Who is on the throne!

If you have turned away from Him, just cry out, and He will bring healing.

If you are in a storm and the waves are about to swamp the boat, look to Him. He will calm the sea. Don't let fear cause you to take your eyes off your King.

The one thing that is certain to change in life is circumstances, which is why the Bible tells us to trust not what we can see, but rather what we can't. The circumstance you are in right now will not last forever, so don't put your faith or your focus on the power of the storm, but in Him who will see you through it.

How Faithful Is He?

Philip and I have a friend named Scott. A former marine, Scott told me that part of the marine creed is never to leave a man behind. Regardless of what might be blowing up around them, and how risky the situation might be, they always go back for their fellow marines.

I saw a movie called *Tears of the Sun*. It was quite a brutal story, but it did illustrate this point. Bruce Willis, as a Navy SEAL, was sent to rescue a medical doctor from an African country before rebel guerrillas got to her. When he arrived, she didn't want to leave the people under her care, but he tricked her into doing so.

Then, as they were flying away and he saw the devastation the guerrillas had brought about, he turned the helicopter around and went back to get the suffering people the doctor had treated. This hadn't been in his initial orders, but he couldn't leave them behind, knowing they would be killed. He got out of his safe helicopter and risked his own life so that he could walk this bunch of wounded men and women to a refugee camp. They all barely made it. That's what added the excitement! (Sorry if I ruined the movie for you!)

While I appreciate Hollywood and certainly Bruce's heroism (☺), that is not even close to the faithfulness of our God. He is "reliable, trustworthy, and therefore ever true to His promise, and He can be depended on." Jesus said that He would *never* leave us . . . never. He is with us right now, in the midst of whatever storms we are fighting.

GOD TO THE RESCUE—EVERY TIME

A man mentioned in the Old Testament had an interesting name: Jehoshaphat. (Anyone got that one in your baby-name books?!) He made it through his storm because he dropped the right anchors and remembered who was on the throne.

At the beginning of this story (2 Chron. 20), Jehoshaphat learned that more than one army was coming to attack him. He was about to enter the storm zone! His first reaction was probably the same as many of ours. He got scared! Very understandable. If you found out that the biggest armies on the planet were coming to get you, you might shake in your boots too!

> WHEN WE GIVE RIGHT HONOR TO GOD, THEN He can move on OUR BEHALF.

While he was feeling just a bit frightened, he went to church. He surrounded himself with the people of God, and he prayed. He reminded God that He was the God of the heavens and ruled over all kingdoms. (As if God needed reminding!) Then he told God about the armies coming against him and said that he had no might to stand against them, but that he knew God did. He let God know that he was looking to Him for deliverance. He remembered Who God was. And God did the coolest thing: He told Jehoshaphat that the upcoming battle was not the king's, but the King's. He wanted Jehoshaphat and his boys just to take their positions, but God would do the fighting for them.

The position that Jehoshaphat took was one of worship. He got the singers together, and while they were worshiping God, the enemies destroyed each other. (I don't think it had to do with the quality of their voices. Remember in *Shrek,* when the princess sang and a bird exploded?! Some voice!) Jehoshaphat didn't have to lift a finger, except to collect the spoil after the battle was over. When we give right honor to God, then He can move on our behalf. We can exalt God or our circumstances—entirely our choice.

Size Never Matters

So, are your problems pretty big? How big are they?

Think about this. Have you ever seen photos of whales? The really big ones? I once saw a photo of a whale with a human next to it—just to give perspective on the whale's actual size. If you saw that photo, you might think, *Those whales are really big.*

Well . . . they aren't really that big when you compare them to the size of a mountain. If you could put one hundred whales in a large container, to make up the size of Mount Everest you would have to fill about one million of those containers. If you were to do that, you'd realize, *Wow, mountains are big, aren't they?*

Well . . . they aren't really that big when you compare them to our planet. When you see a satellite photo of Earth taken from outer space, the highest of mountains looks like a speck of sand. You might think, *Our planet is really big, isn't it?*

Well . . . it isn't really if you compare it to, say, the sun. It would take about one million planet Earths to match the size of the sun. *That's amazing. The sun is really big, isn't it?*

Well . . . it isn't really that big if you compare it to some of the stars in the galaxy. One of the stars in the galaxy is so enormous that it would take fifty million of our sun to match its size. *Now, that is a very big star.*

Well . . . not really, if you consider that this is one star in a galaxy in which there are billions of stars. *All righty, then. The galaxy is massive, isn't it?*

Well . . . not really, because there are billions of galaxies. There are enough galaxies out there that every human on Earth could have at least four of them—four galaxies. Whew!

So the universe must be pretty big, then. And to think that our God created it just by saying the words "Let there be stars and galaxies."

Okay, so now how big is your problem? Is it really too big for God?

Your Destiny Is at Stake

Your storm might be huge. But no one wants you delivered from this storm more than your heavenly Father! God saved Paul and the ship's crew from certain death because He had a purpose for them. In the same way, He has plans for your life beyond the storm.

When oceans rise
and thunders roar
I will soar with you
above the storm
Father, you are King
over the flood
I will be still and know
that you are God.

—Reuben Morgan[1]

nine

WHAT TO DO WITH THE STORMS WE STIR UP OURSELVES

The movie *Twister* was certainly entertaining. Maybe because I don't live in the tornado zone, I could watch it and not take any of it personally! (The flying cows were a little weird, though!) Don't get me started about the movie *Earthquake*—that's a little too close to home. What was interesting to me about *Twister* was that the scientists had all of this incredible equipment that they used to chase storms: not avoid them, but seek them out. They risked their lives, looking for tornadoes. I know they hoped to figure out what caused them so they could predict them . . . but still, they were *hunting down storms*. Now, maybe we aren't chasing twisters, but some of us bring storms on ourselves because of the choices we make. Does one of the following describe you?

Maybe you are in a financial storm because you have

consistently spent more than you earn. It won't take too many months of this spending pattern to create a storm!

Maybe you had sex with someone, and it turns out he had an STD. Now you do too. Serious storm.

Maybe you had a few drinks before you left for home. Only you didn't make it home. A policeman stopped you, and now you are the proud owner of a DUI ticket and all that involves. Or perhaps you had an accident while under the influence, broke your legs, and hurt someone else too. Pretty bad storm.

Maybe, while your husband was out of town, you casually went out to dinner with someone from the office. Now you find yourself attracted to him and wonder if you ever were really in love with your husband. This new man seems so much more exciting . . . Or maybe you simply stopped investing the necessary time into building your relationship with your husband. Either way—marriage storm.

Maybe you were so lonely that you married the first guy who asked. Never mind that he didn't know God, still prefers to party with his single guy friends, and can't keep a job. Now you find yourself in a storm, because you said "I do" when you should have said "I don't"!

Maybe you had an abortion or two, and now you are dealing with the hurt in your heart. Sad storm.

Maybe you did so many drugs that you lost your family—a tragic storm.

Maybe you have smoked for years and now have emphysema or lung cancer. Life-threatening storm.

Maybe junk food has been your staple for years and you are now two hundred pounds overweight: dangerous health storm.

Sometimes we make foolish choices and have to eat the fruit of them. Bad decisions yield bad results, no matter whom we try to blame. Getting through a mess we have created for ourselves is one of the most difficult storms to weather. We have all been in this kind of storm at one time or another.[2]

Big Waves, Big Fish

A man named Jonah certainly found himself in a storm, one based on his decision to disobey God. Most of us know the story. His storm—which included a visit to the belly of a big fish—came because he abandoned God's plan for him. Rather than choose to accept his divine assignment to go to Nineveh, he headed for Tarshish. Nineveh is where modern-day Iraq and Iran are, and Tarshish was basically a resort town. Hmmm . . . tough choice! Iran/Iraq or the beach? No wonder Jonah chose what he did. Only thing is, God didn't send him to the beach; God sent him to an area that needed to know Him.

We may not always like where God sends us. And there may be times when we want out: of our marriage, our church, our city. But leaving our divine assignment will always create a storm. Abandoning the purpose for which God created us will always start trouble. Maybe not a three-day stay inside a big fish—but definitely trouble! (Just warning you!)

And a sobering thought, which I explained more fully in Chapter 6, is that Jonah's decision to disobey God and abandon his assignment impacted others: the ones with him (who would have drowned if Jonah had stayed in the boat), and the ones who weren't hearing God's warning to repent because Jonah wasn't where he was supposed to be. The storms we stir up ourselves always hurt others as well as ourselves.

> LEAVING OUR DIVINE ASSIGNMENT WILL ALWAYS CREATE A STORM.

Maybe you are looking at your life right now and thinking, *Boy, am I in a mess!* Are you wondering how you got there? Most of us have heard the story of the prodigal son. He found himself in a mess (a pigpen, to be exact), and he asked himself the same question. *How did this happen? What caused this storm?*

You may have more in common with him than you thought.

THE PRODIGAL SON: STEPS TO A STORM

STEP 1: FEELING ENTITLED

The prodigal son's first mistake: he began to feel entitled. He felt the world owed him something. As a young man, he wanted to untie the apron strings and strike out on his own. Not an unusual desire for a young man—but he wanted to use his inheritance as a springboard. Like Jonah, he decided to make his own plans. Maybe home life was getting too hard: he was tired of doing what others wanted him to do, or maybe his older brother was bothering him. Who knows? Basically he said, "I want what's mine, and I want it *now!*"

The money would one day have indeed been his. He was supposed to receive his inheritance at the right time—which would have been at his father's death. Until then, he was supposed to be helping his father, being faithful to help build and support another man's vision. Then he would have been entrusted with his own.

Instead, he wanted it now. Why? He felt he was entitled to it. This is the first step toward creating a storm: feeling as if someone owes us something.

Perhaps you feel that your boss owes you a bigger salary, so you grumble at work. I am not saying you can't ask for a raise, if you think it is appropriate. But the attitude of "You owe me" will only create a storm in your workplace.

Maybe you are a phenomenal keyboard player in your church band. You think you are so good, the church leadership ought to put your name in the bulletin, or put the piano center stage. You are headed for a storm. There will always be people around to feed your ego, saying, "You are so good, Miss Piano Player. You deserve your own spotlight!" Don't listen.

If you are married and think that because you pick up your husband's laundry and cook dinner, he owes you . . . you are headed for a storm. Remember when you were first dating and glad to do things for him? You didn't look for much in return—just his company. Now you are keeping IOUs. Be careful! (A tip for free: A better mind-set would be that your spouse owes you absolutely nothing for all the things you have done; you've done them because you chose to—humbly and happily.)

STEP 2: BECOMING SELF-INDULGENT

The second step the prodigal took on his way to creating a storm—and the second step you and I take on our journeys toward trouble—is that he began to be incredibly self-indulgent. Self-indulgence is thinking *me . . . me . . . me!* This is when we do anything to satisfy every desire we have. Maybe because the prodigal was the younger son, he wanted to feel important, so he left home and spent his money on parties and prostitutes. This guy was out blowing his inheritance on fancy clothes, fancy women, and a fancy house—all to satisfy a need. When we begin to feel that people owe us and then try to satisfy that feeling with self-indulgence, we are headed for rough water.

A SELF-INDULGENT PERSON HAS LOST SIGHT OF HER TRUE IDENTITY. SHE HAS FORGOTTEN SHE IS A CHILD OF THE KING, CREATED WITH A PURPOSE AND DESTINED TO WIN.

If you are married and begin to think, "I deserve sex whenever I want" or "I deserve to be understood, and I am not getting it here, so I'll look elsewhere," you are sailing into stormy seas. Trying to fulfill our desires through extramarital flings—or eating too much or spending money we shouldn't—is a disastrous choice.

A self-indulgent person has lost sight of her true identity.

She has forgotten she is a child of the King, created with a purpose and destined to win. And the self-indulgent woman is usually the last to notice it. It is pretty obvious, though: the self-indulgent person doesn't care about anyone else.

As a child of the King, I am to serve humanity. I am to focus on using what God has given me to help someone else. My friend Bobbie said, "The kingdom of God is about me and yet not about me." That is so true. Jesus came so that you and I could live an incredible life, free from the chains that bind. So, yes, it is about us. And yet, it is not about us. The lives He has given us, we are supposed to give away. Self-indulgent people are too busy taking time to "find themselves" to help anyone. This is one way you can tell you are stirring up a storm: What have you done for anyone else lately?

STEP 3: ABANDONING THE PEOPLE YOU ARE ASSIGNED TO

The third thing the prodigal son did to create a storm was to leave the people who loved and supported him. When he departed from his lifelong home, he left accountability. In his immaturity, he left wisdom, perhaps because he felt it was limiting. Immaturity usually doesn't recognize wise words or people. Rather than receiving correction and being willing to change, he just decided to leave.

God did not design you and me to do

GOD DID NOT DESIGN YOU AND ME TO DO LIFE ALONE, APART FROM WISE COUNSEL.

life alone, apart from wise counsel. When we separate ourselves not only from God, but also from the people He has planted in our lives, we're in trouble. We will grow and flourish only when we are connected to each other.

Maybe you feel so bad about choices you've made that shame drives you away. *Don't let it!!* You will only face an even greater storm. Perhaps someone in church hurt your feelings, and rather than getting over the offense, you chose to leave the very people God sent to help you grow and heal. Maybe you cloak your leaving in religious terms—"I just need to be alone with God"—when what you really want is to get away from where someone holds you accountable. *Stop!* God set up a safeguard system for us, and it's called Each Other.

One of the greatest friendships recorded in the Bible was between Jonathan and David. They were both warriors, pursuing the cause of their God. In 1 Samuel we read that their souls were knit together. That's a pretty tight friendship! As Saul's son, Jonathan would have been next in line to be king, but God didn't see it that way. Because of Saul's disobedience, He had taken Saul's kingdom from him and given it to David. This didn't seem to bother Jonathan, who was very committed to David. He realized that his friendship with David was more important than accomplishments or stuff. (We should all learn that! People should always be more important than material gain or promotion. After all, the stuff isn't entering eternity with you!)

Jonathan and David encouraged one another . . . they spoke well of one another . . . they laughed and cried with each other.

You know, all of the things friends are supposed to do together.

One day, however, Jonathan decided that he needed to go fight by his father's side. He should have been with David, but instead he got sentimental over his father, who had gone astray, and went to him. By this time, his father had tried to kill David numerous times, had consulted a witch, and basically had turned from God, so Jonathan had no business being with his father. During this trip to his father, he was killed.

I can't prove it, but I don't think it should have happened. I think he should have lived a long time as one of David's generals. After all, he had pledged himself to David. But he left the friendship—the relationship that was a strength—and ended up dying. When we separate ourselves from the people we are assigned to, we are on our way to a mess!

STEP 4: CHOOSING BAD COMPANY

On this road to a storm, the prodigal son separated himself from God and the people who loved him. The story tells us that after he had spent all his money, there was a famine in the land. A famine is a season of scarcity, deprivation, and shortage. We have all endured periods of lack—in finances, peace, vision, or hope. Famines are scary. They seem endless.

In his need, the young man began to work for a citizen of that country. He joined himself to someone who didn't know God or anything about following Him. We know this because he owned pigs—an animal the Jews believed was unclean. And that man sent the prodigal to feed his herd. To a Jew, this would have to be the most disgusting job possible. (Actually, I think it's pretty disgusting too!)

This fourth step toward a storm of our own making comes when we join ourselves with someone who doesn't know God. Someone who doesn't know Him or His Word can't help us back on the right path. I am not saying that we shouldn't spend time with people who are not believers. Jesus visited with all sorts of people. The difference is that Jesus was a blessing to the people He met; they were a part of His divine assignment. When we are running from God and choose the company of people who don't serve Him, rarely are we a blessing to them. All we do is bring our storm into their lives. Jonah brought the storm onto the people on the ship. He was definitely not a blessing to them!

Because these people have no reverence for God, we begin to pick up some of their habits. We do some unclean things. The shame is terrible. The unworthiness we feel is awful, and the devil laughs at how successful his plan of leading us into a storm was.

When we're in a storm, we might settle for things we never would otherwise. We settle for pig slop until even it begins to look good.

I have known a few young women who came to church, began relationships with God, and really seemed to be on the right path. Then some of their friends got married, and they began to feel just a little

> WHEN we're in a storm, we might settle for things we never would otherwise. We settle for pig slop until even it begins to look good.

envious. (You know—that old green monster attacks again!) What if you find out that a friend, who has been single (but not for nearly as long as you have), is getting married? Can you be happy, truly happy for her? Or do you feel things like . . .

- Hey, *I'm* the one who went to Jenny Craig and lost all of this weight!!
- What's the deal? *I'm* the one who had my eyeliner and lips tattooed for around-the-clock beauty!
- *I'm* the one who's spent hours learning about football!
- *I* even took classes on relinquishing the remote control!
- What's up with this? I should be getting married next! *I'm* the one who's been a bridesmaid seventeen times!

If you do find yourself feeling jealous, it should be an indication to you of a slight sense of insecurity, and perhaps a hint that you aren't trusting your Father. He is not going to withhold good from you!

These women I knew gave in to these feelings and decided to leave the church, because obviously God wasn't supplying mates. They felt God owed them, and they gave into self-indulgence. They left the place where they were being made strong. Some of them left the city and the country in their quest for a mate.

Is it wrong to want a husband? *No!* But the way we choose to meet our needs can be. When we stay on the path of our purpose, God will always take care of us. He is under no obligation to meet or finance needs when we step outside of His will.

These women let the desire for a man dominate all else. Rather than continue to work on the issues of their hearts, they decided to focus on a husband hunt.

One of these women attached herself to someone she never should have. In her desire to end her loneliness, she began a relationship with a man who was controlling and emotionally abusive. And in her desperation, she stayed with him. (A tip for free: Another person is never a lasting cure for loneliness. Many married people are lonely. We end loneliness when we let God into the empty places in our hearts.) She got pregnant, then felt so guilty that she married him. Now she is bringing a child into her storm.

Another of the women still has not found a husband. She left the house of God, where she was being challenged to grow and work on her issues, and she is now isolated. The unresolved hurts in her past continue to come up in very sad ways, thus making her unattractive to any healthy man. She continues to experience financial difficulties. Who knows what would have happened if she had stayed connected to the House?

Some people I heard about used drugs to counteract their sense of worthlessness. They worked hard at their jobs, so they felt it was their right to have a little fun with cocaine . . . you know, just to take the edge off a tough day. They were convinced that they were not addicted—they could handle it. It wasn't long, though, before they had to have a little coke in the middle of the day—just to help them deal with daily pressures. Then their habits got really expensive, and they spent most of their money on the drugs.

Compounding the problem, they lied about where the money was going. They lost their jobs, their families, their homes, and most of their friends . . . all because they started with a feeling of being owed something, and they began to fill that need with self-indulgent behavior. Soon they were out on the street or living in hovels, spending time with other addicts and dealers. They attached themselves to people who only pulled them further down. A very serious storm of their own making.

Some people move to Los Angeles to become famous. The sad truth is that most never will. There have been people who have come to the church looking for fame, for significance. Some have gotten frustrated when people's recognition didn't come quickly enough. Our significance will never come from the applause of men. It comes when we understand that we are the loved-beyond-measure daughters of a King.

The need to feel significant is not a bad one . . . again, it is how we choose to meet it. A few people have left churches where they were receiving help, where they were learning to become people of integrity, simply because they weren't handed center stage quickly enough. Like the prodigal son, they wanted their inheritance, and they wanted it *now!* They began to feel they were owed something.

Jesus challenged us to be faithful with what is another man's, because by doing this, we kill the self-indulgent behavior that can mess up our lives. A few of the people who have left the church are now just wandering souls, looking for a purpose. They are having financial problems, they have lost the respect of many of their peers, and they still haven't achieved the fame they were seeking. They are in storms of their own making. It is so unnecessary that it just breaks my heart.

Many try to satisfy the hurts in their hearts by spending money . . . lots of it . . . money they don't have. They have a bad day, week, year, whatever, and they figure they deserve a little fun. Out comes the credit card. They shop and shop. They reject any financial counseling. Or maybe they try to fill their needs by gambling away money. Then they find themselves thousands of dollars in debt, and they have to link themselves to some not-nice people to get loans.

Many people, feeling they are owed love and affection, try to satisfy that need in all sorts of perverted ways. The need for love is a universal one, and we are sexual beings, but we need to meet those needs in a marriage that we are committed to working on, not by seeking different sexual partners. We need to learn love from our Creator.

The Way Home from a Storm

We know from Scripture that the prodigal didn't stay with the pigs. We can take a few lessons from his journey from the sty to security.

Lesson 1: Come to Your Senses

Shame lies at the end of the storm. The prodigal son was ashamed as he found himself—the son of a very wealthy man—envying pigs. (And most of the people I've just described were ashamed when they saw what they had done.) He finally came to his senses. He realized that even the servants in his father's house had a better life than he did. (Well, duh!) The pig slop started looking like—you guessed it—pig slop! He knew there was something else—something better. He remembered his father and his old life, not just to reminisce, but to do something about it.

The way to ride through the storms we stir up ourselves is the same as with any other storm—except first, we have to deal with any guilt we might be feeling. Feelings of guilt and shame are universal and can destroy our souls. "When guilt takes hold, we become fixated on past sins and mistakes. We begin to live life in the rearview mirror—no longer seeing life's opportunities before us because we are blinded by a past full of what 'would have been, could have been and should have been.'"[3]

If we look around and find ourselves in the pigpen—a storm of our own making—we need to stir ourselves up to take action. We can't settle for what we have. If you realize that you are not living the life God has promised, which is an overcoming, abundant, confetti-throwing, parade-riding life, then you *must* come to your senses! Jesus paid a great price for us to live incredible lives! Take your hand, smack yourself on the cheek, and say, "Self, wake up!"

LESSON 2: GET HUMBLE

After we come to our senses, the next thing we have to do to get out of our self-made storm is humble ourselves. Yuck! The prodigal son realized that he was going to have to do this before his father. He prepared himself to say, "Father, I blew it. I know I am not even worthy to be called your son, so I will come back as a servant."

I am not talking about the humbling that life does for us, but rather the decision to humble ourselves and admit fault or failure. Not so easy for most of us! Life *can* take us down a notch, though! I heard a story about a pastor who officiated at a funeral and then was supposed to lead the funeral procession to the cemetery. Well, he got a bit distracted as he was driving (maybe he had a touch of ADD!), and he pulled into a Wal-Mart parking lot, thinking about something he needed to pick up. He looked in his rearview mirror and noticed that a string of cars was following him into the parking lot—all with their lights on! Oops!!

In the 1980s, I was working as an actress in Los Angeles. One of my first jobs in television was as a lead character in a nighttime soap opera (you know, one of those really educational shows!!). I was supposed to be the pretty, young female heart-throb in the show . . . which basically meant I was in a bikini or lingerie the entire time! I was a bit nervous because this was my first really big part. As I was being fitted for wardrobe and the different skimpy outfits I would wear, the producers decided that my figure was not curvy enough. To remedy this situation, they had the wardrobe people place mastectomy pads in my bikini top. (Now you know a Hollywood secret!)

The first scene I was to film involved a conflict between my stepfather and me. We were at the beach, and after our fight, I was to get away from him by running down the beach with my dog. I took off running, cameras were rolling—when one of the mastectomy pads flew out of my bikini top and fell to the sand. I stopped. The dog stopped. I looked at the pad in the sand. The dog looked at the pad in the sand. I knew at that moment that I could have laughed, cried, or been mad at the wardrobe people for not sewing the pad into the bikini top. I chose to laugh. The director yelled, "Cut!" Wardrobe people came over to remedy the situation, which involved a needle and thread! Was I embarrassed? Yes . . . and definitely slightly humbled!

Just last week I was speaking at a conference. I'm sure I was right in the middle of a brilliant point (☺) when I stepped right off of the stage into thin air!! I bet the cameraman who was taping the conference wondered where I went. I picked myself up, laughed, and climbed back on the stage. Just a little humbling! There really is no fear of my ever getting too big for my britches!

So, yes, life does do some things that can humiliate us. But that is *not* what I am talking about. The Bible challenges us to humble ourselves. Bill Hybels says that people already know we make mistakes; they want to know if we have the integrity to admit them.

In his book with Ken Blanchard, *Everyone's a Coach,* Don Shula wrote of losing his temper near an open microphone during a televised game with the Los Angeles Rams. Shula's explicit profanity shocked millions of viewers. He received letters from all over the country. Fans had admired him, and now they questioned his character. Shula could have given excuses; most people would have. But he didn't. He sent a personal apology to everyone who had written. He closed the letters by saying, "I value your respect, and will do my best to earn it again."[4] He created a storm, and he began his journey out by humbling himself.

So, if you find yourself in a storm of your own making, you can start escaping it by coming to your senses, then by humbling yourself. Admit you were wrong. Say you're sorry. Admit responsibility for hurting the people around you. Avoid getting defensive, or you will find yourself right back in the pigpen!

LESSON 3: REPENT

The next thing the prodigal son did as he was working himself out of his storm was repent. *Repent* means to turn and move in the opposite direction. He had to move; otherwise, he would have stayed in the sty, feeling humiliated. Repentance involves making decisions that head you in the right way—not just saying "I'm sorry," but *changing*.

If you have made financial decisions that have hurt your family, saying "I'm sorry" isn't enough. You must begin to adjust how you handle money. If your lifestyle has produced a weak and unhealthy body, feeling sorry about it is not enough. You must choose different foods and start to exercise.

In 2 Samuel 11–12, we learn that David, who was known as a man after God's own heart, found himself in a serious storm of his own making. In the spring, when good weather once again came to Israel, all the kings were to go out and check on their borders—make sure no enemies had crossed over during the winter months. David knew this was what he should do—this is what *all* kings did—but the Bible tells us that while other kings were inspecting their borders, David decided to stay home. He sent Joab in his place. Not a good decision.

Then we find out that one evening, David got up from his bed and walked around on the roof of his palace. What was he doing, getting out of bed in the evening? I guess with nothing to do all day, he just stayed in bed. Bad decision. So, of course, he was not tired in the evening because he hadn't done much all day. While he was in the place he shouldn't have been in, he saw something he shouldn't have seen.

He saw a beautiful woman on the roof next door, taking a bath. (I just want to know how she got the bathtub up to the roof?!) David didn't know who she was (he must not have been very neighborly!), so he sent his servants to check her out. She must have been better looking than the average next-door neighbor to get his attention, because David was not lacking for women: he had a palace full of them. He found out the woman was Bathsheba and that she was married to one of his soldiers.

This didn't stop him from bringing her to the palace and having sex with her. Not a good decision. First, David was in a place he shouldn't have been, then he looked where he shouldn't have been looking, he saw something he shouldn't have seen, and then he did something he shouldn't have done.

Well, a few weeks later, while all of the men were still at war, Bathsheba told David that she was pregnant. Then he had a serious mess. There was no way she could tell her husband that the baby was his, because he had been off to war for months. So, David started a cover-up—which ended up being worse than the original sin. He sent for Uriah, Bathsheba's husband.

David didn't know Uriah; they were not friends, and I'm sure Uriah thought it was strange that the king had summoned him home. He went before the king, and David asked him how Joab, the general was doing; he asked him how the soldiers were doing; and he asked him, a lowly soldier, how the war was going. I'm sure Uriah wondered what in the world he was doing there.

But we know that David didn't bring Uriah home just to chat about the war. Then David said, "You have come a long way, Uriah. You should go home, take a shower, and see your wife." And he gave him a present to take with him. David had a plan. He wanted Uriah to have sex with Bathsheba so that the baby could be passed off as Uriah's. David thought he was very clever. He was sure that his plan would work.

Boy, wasn't David surprised when he found out that Uriah did not go see his wife. Uriah said that he couldn't be with his wife when the rest of the soldiers were at war, camping in the fields. David had not planned on encountering a man of integrity. The next day, David tried to get him drunk, so that maybe then he would go to his wife. David was not looking like a great king at this point. But once again, Uriah refused. He couldn't do it while his fellow Israelites were in battle.

Then David had to resort to Plan B. The next day he sent Uriah back to the battle with a note to give Joab. The note instructed Joab to place Uriah at the front lines, then pull the other soldiers back . . . thus ensuring Uriah's death. David was, in fact, a murderer. Not only was he an adulterer, but he was responsible for someone's death. He was in a real storm.

David went from being in the wrong place, to looking where he shouldn't look, to taking what was not his to take, to trying to deny his sin, to trying to compromise a fellow Israelite, to murdering.

David then married Bathsheba, and she gave birth to a son. It appeared that David got away with his actions . . . but the Bible tells us that God was not pleased with the king's actions. God sent the prophet Nathan to David. Nathan told the king a story of two men: a rich man who had many flocks and herds, and a poor one who had only one lamb. The poor man loved his lamb; it was like a daughter to him. He fed it from his own table and took good care of it. The rich man had a visitor and wanted to fix a nice dinner for him. Rather than taking one of his own sheep and killing it for dinner, he took the only one the poor man had—and slaughtered it.

David was so angry with the rich man when he heard this story that he said he was worthy of death. Nathan told David that the rich man was David himself. David was a wealthy man whom God had richly blessed, and yet he had taken Uriah's only wife and then had Uriah killed. I'm sure David was surprised to find out that his storm, which he thought no one knew about, was now public. David did make the right response, though. Rather than coming up with excuses and being angry, he admitted his sin and repented before God.

David brought about this storm himself. But like the prodigal son, he did come to his senses, recognize his sin, and repent.

Welcome Back!

The prodigal son found that as he took these steps to get out of his mess, his father was waiting for him. *I love that!* While the son was still quite a distance away from home, the father saw him and ran to him. God is like that. He is looking for us as we turn back to Him. He is the God of the second and third and fourth chances! Our friend Jonah found this out too. After he humbled himself in the belly of the fish, the fish vomited him out onto a beach. (Yuck!) Then he heard God say again to go to Nineveh. God's assignment for Jonah hadn't changed. His assignment for you hasn't either. You just get another chance to do it right!

The father hugged and kissed the son; he didn't say, "I told you so." He gave him a robe, sandals, and a ring. He couldn't give him back the years, though. That is the sad part. We will never get back the time we waste in our self-inflicted storm. The word *prodigal* actually means *wasteful,* and the young man certainly was wasteful with money but also, more importantly, with time. We should be making the most of the days, weeks, and months we have on Earth!

> GOD'S ASSIGNMENT FOR JONAH HADN'T CHANGED. HIS ASSIGNMENT FOR YOU HASN'T EITHER.

Philip knew that God called him into the ministry when he was about twenty. Well, that did not sound like something he wanted to do, so he spent the next decade running from God: doing drugs, making bad decisions, and basically just wasting his life. He finally came to his senses and back to the Father. One of his big passions now is to help young people know and fulfill their purpose, so that they won't waste their years. (He just turned fifty this year, and he is the coolest and best-looking fifty-year-old I know. I think God is helping him to stay young-looking because he is behind a decade!! ☺)

Enjoy the Party!

The father was so glad to see his prodigal son come home that he threw a party for him. This is not only the response God has when we turn to Him (He loves parties!), but this should be our response when people we know and love are on their journeys out of self-created messes. The words "I told you so" should not be in our vocabulary! The truth is, most of us have been in a storm of our own making at one time or another. We don't want to be judged; we want to be loved and embraced as we come home. So, I do want to take a few moments to challenge those in the church to have the attitude of the Father as people are coming home.

Let's say that we know someone whose life is a wreck. We'll call her Ann. She is doing drugs, getting drunk every week, having sex with just about any man who'll have her, weighs 380 pounds, is angry and bitter toward men because of the abuse of her childhood, hates her mother for abandoning her, and cusses like a sailor (no offense to all of you sailors!). She is in the midst of a very chaotic storm.

Some brave person looks beyond the mess and introduces her to her Savior. Ann says yes to a relationship with her Creator and is now on the journey home. I don't know about you, but when I first said yes to God, all of the issues in my life didn't just go away; I had to do a little work. So does Ann.

She is at what I call Door Number One: just a saved mess . . . so very, very loved by her God . . . on her way to heaven . . . but still a mess! (And unless she works on some things, she will probably go to heaven before she is supposed to!) You see, God doesn't love us more the longer we follow Him. He loves us unconditionally—even while we reject Him. He loves us when we make bad choices, and when we make good ones. His love never changes.

Once we say yes to Him, we are on the journey called "working out our salvation." We can park ourselves at Door Number One and never move, if that's what we choose. If we do that, however, we will probably die before our time—and God doesn't need us dead. If He did, we would all be in heaven, singing with the angels. He needs us alive and well on the planet, fulfilling the purpose for which He created us. He needs us to live. He needs Ann to live. He has a purpose for her to fulfill.

So, God begins to talk to Ann. She goes to church, and maybe the pastor, who has never said anything about drugs, throws a sentence in his sermon about the dangers of cocaine. She doesn't think too much about it, until she gets home and turns on her TV. The program is all about how many people have overdosed on drugs this year. She quickly shuts it off. Then she gets a phone call from an old friend, who tells her of some serious health problems he is suffering from drug use; he is now in the hospital with little hope. She wonders just what is going on! Is God trying to give her a rule to follow? Is serving God all about the rules? *No!!* God loves her and needs her to live. Drugs kill.

Perhaps she says, "Okay, God, I will try it Your way. I will stop using." And God applauds her, saying, "Way to go, honey!" (Well, that's how He talks to me!!) He lets her rest in this victory. But soon He begins to talk to her about the next step on her journey. Remember, it is not about the rules: it's about living to fulfill destiny!

Maybe now God begins to challenge her about sleeping around. The truth is, it is a toss-up what will kill you first: sleeping around or doing drugs. We have buried people who caught diseases from having sex with partners they shouldn't have. And don't believe the world when it tells you that condoms can keep you from getting any sexually transmitted diseases—they can't.

God is not trying to take away Ann's fun. He is wanting her to *live.* He wants her body and heart to be whole and healthy.

Ann watches another TV show about all of the thousands of sexually transmitted diseases that are out there. Then a friend calls Ann and tells her that she just got back from the doctor. She just found out that she will never be able to have children because of an STD she contracted in her younger days. Ann goes to church, and the pastor reads a Scripture that challenges people to avoid fornication. Ann decides that she hasn't been involved in fornication—no, she's making love. That's different! (Ever notice how we try to justify our sins?!) She eventually does yield to God's way, however. After all, her way has brought only pain.

And again, God celebrates her choice. He doesn't love her any more now than He did before she said yes to Him; she just has a better chance of living long enough to fulfill His purpose for her.

To me, life is a series of doors that we walk through. In the beginning of our walk, God is dealing with the issues that are, perhaps, evident to all. Eventually, however, maybe at Door Number Twenty-seven, He begins to deal with the issues of the heart. Because things like unforgiveness will kill—maybe not as quickly as a needle in the arm—but they will kill. At some doors, we must let go of things, and at others, we take on things, like a marriage, a job, a move—whatever is part of our destiny.

My challenge to those of you who have been on this journey for a while is: don't forget what you looked like when you started! Some people, who might be at Door Number Eighty-six, look at the people who are at Door Number One—just starting their journeys home—and they judge them. They say things like "Could that skirt get any shorter, honey?? Is that cigarette smoke I smell on your breath? And did you just curse in church? What's the matter with you?"

Family, our job is not to judge those on the journey, but to love and embrace . . . to give them a robe and throw a party as they come. We are to cheer their steps toward home—not judge.

———————————

If you find yourself in a storm of your own making, take the steps to get yourself out. And, if you are watching someone climb out of her mess, give her a hand up, not an "I told you so." Then, enjoy the party God the Father throws!

come on honey

No lower value could I place
On me, the one I am.
My dreams as insignificant,
No bigger than a seed.

Two hands beckon me forward
Come on Honey
Grow

I try to get up and find,
I have fallen further.
By a chain I drag my past,
Close behind me.

Two hands beckon me forward
Come on Honey
Let go

Challenged, to run my race
That started long ago.
Gasps of surrender, I am the whiner
Slumped under the tree of hardship.

Two hands beckon me forward
Come on Honey
Stretch

I look up, knowing from Heaven
He looks down, in His arms I'm found.
"Honey, you're mine"
He says wiping the tear from my eye.
"In Me you can do it all."

—KATHLEEN DEACON

some last
thoughts as we
reach shore

The God we serve is a good God. Still, we live in a world where good and evil exist together. When challenges and storms come our way, we get to choose how we react. God did not create us as puppets; we have a choice. Will we let the trial refine us, or define us? Will we be committed to getting through it victoriously, or will we sink? The choice is entirely ours.

In the preceding pages, I hope I have presented practical steps we can all take as we make our way through the storm. And here I want to repeat the reason we *must* make it through: generations are counting on us. The trial, if we let it, can bring out the best in us: "endurance and steadfastness and patience." As the diamond is revealed only after the piece of coal has been under pressure, the treasure in us can be exposed when the storm hits. And those around us will benefit as we do.

In the seventeenth century, John Bunyan wrote *Pilgrim's Progress* from a prison cell. One of the best-selling books of all time came from an author's serious storm. Martin Luther King Jr. wrote *Letters from a Birmingham Jail* while he was in captivity. During World War II, Dietrich Bonhoeffer's *Letters and Papers from Prison* emerged from his sojourn behind bars. In the midst of challenge and adversity, treasure appeared.

True to His word, God saved Paul and all those on the ship. No lives were lost. The ship, however, did not fare quite as well! The storm shattered it. After you get through the storm you are in, you probably will be stronger, and thus you will also be a different "vessel" for the next part of your journey. Who you were got you to the place you are now, but you will need to be stronger to finish your journey!

Paul and the others made shore by hanging on to boards and swimming for all they were worth. Once there, they recognized the island of Malta—not their original destination. I'm sure neither Paul nor the sailors had a plan that included Malta . . . but God did. People on that island needed to have an encounter with the living God, and Paul was just the guy to bring it about. Getting through the storm had a higher purpose!

There are people on your shore, too, who need the life of God that is in you. God is not looking down at you and me in our storms and feeling sorry for us. No! He is looking way down the road He has called us to travel. He sees a whole bunch of people He needs us to touch with His love. After all, we are His hands. So, maybe you are feeling a bit weak and whiney (we've all been there), because you are in a storm or you think the storm has knocked you off course. Nope. You are in His hands. If you open your eyes, you will see lots of people around you waiting for you to get up.

The prophet Elijah did a fairly incredible thing. He defeated the prophets of Baal in a big demonstration of the power of God. There had been a drought in the land because the people had turned from God to worship Baal. In order to challenge the prophets of Baal, Elijah told them they were going to have a contest. They both built altars and placed bulls on them. Elijah told the prophets of Baal to cry out to their god and see if he would consume the sacrifice. The prophets of Baal frantically called on their god—to no avail. Elijah was even feeling so confident that he taunted them, saying, "Oh, maybe your God is asleep!"

Then Elijah, feeling particularly sure of himself, dumped lots of water on his altar, called on his God—the God of Abraham, Isaac, and Jacob—and fire came from heaven, consuming the sacrifice. Then Elijah proceeded to slaughter the prophets of Baal. Shortly after that, he prophesied to Ahab the king that it would begin to rain—and it did. So, Elijah had quite a day! Quite a victory.

The next day Jezebel, Ahab's wife, sent a note to Elijah, saying that she was going to kill him. This freaked out Elijah so much that he ran. He had just killed hundreds of prophets, called fire out of heaven, and accurately predicted rain—and then he ran from a note?! He journeyed into the desert, lay down, and told God to kill him. He had had enough.

Twice, God sent an angel to him to feed and comfort him. Then Elijah traveled forty days and hid in a cave. He started telling God that he was the only man of God left, and he should just die. Elijah was whining. I can hear God sigh. Do you think God sighs on occasion? He calmly told Elijah that no, there were seven thousand who had not bowed to Baal, and that Elijah was to go back the way he came. God was not finished with him yet.

Elijah did some pretty important things after this moment—but first, he had to get up and get back on track. There were people he had to touch. Same for you and me.

When my marriage was at its stormiest, and I was complaining about Philip to God, I was sure He felt sorry for me. I was sure He could see just how hard I had it. There were moments during this time when I feared I had married the wrong man. (Most of us have thought that at one time or another!) Had I messed up my destiny??

I finally realized that God wasn't feeling sorry for me at all. He was ever present, ever ready, and ever willing to get me through the storm. I'm sure God was sighing, waiting for me to get to the shore, because He had other struggling couples He needed me to help.

I know a number of girls with eating disorders. When I speak with them, most eventually want to help other young women from ending up doing what they did. Yes. That is the right response. They owe it to the girls on their shore to get there. God is waiting, and He is looking at where He called you to go. (If you are in this storm right now, please get some help. You can make it. My friend Nancy Alcorn wrote a book called *Mercy for Eating Disorders.* It can be a huge help in your reaching the shore.)

Paul challenged us: "Be strengthened," or perfected, completed, made what you ought to be. Trials and storms have a way of doing this. God is making my marriage what it ought to be because Philip and I are riding out our storms. God is developing me into a strong parent because I haven't abandoned my children, either emotionally or physically (no matter how tempting!). I am weathering the parenting storms. I have friendships today that God is beautifying because we didn't give up on each other when things got a little uncomfortable. My faith is taking its ordained shape because sometimes I believe in God and His plans—against all odds. I just keep believing and my faith grows stronger.

Storms will come in waves, so hang in there until the calm comes!

Paul and the boys made it to shore, by the way. They were catching their breath and drying off, resting by a fire the natives provided. All of a sudden, a snake crawled out of the pieces of wood in the fire and bit Paul's hand. (As if he hadn't suffered enough!?) First of all, he was a prisoner, then he was on a ship for weeks, going through a dark, horrible storm, then the ship crashed, he had to swim to shore . . . and then, a snake had the nerve to bite him! (Have you ever felt like that? Just when you think all the bad stuff that's going to happen is over—then *wham,* here comes another hit!)

I have watched boxing once or twice. I have to say, I don't really see the point—two men fighting over a "purse"—but whatever! I noticed that the fighters will throw a one-two punch, and the defender might avoid that. But it is the third hit, which seems to come from nowhere, that can knock a fighter out. We do have an enemy on this planet, who is doing whatever he can to knock us off course. If the third hit will do it, then he will deliver it.

Paul handled his third hit, the snakebite, with his usual cool style. He just flicked the snake off. Of course, it freaked out everyone watching. But not Paul. He was not going to let a snake do to him what a storm and a shipwreck couldn't! We need to have a little of that tenacity.

A few years ago, I talked with a married couple going through a storm. In their early twenties, they had not been wise financially and so were evicted from a few apartments. Perhaps they didn't realize that the eviction would stay on their record for quite a while. Five years later, they were staying with family, and while they appreciated the hospitality, they really would have liked an apartment of their own. This couple had three children, and along with his brother's family, they were all living in a three-bedroom apartment in a bad neighborhood. Not a great situation.

She was really getting frustrated. Recently, both of them

had started to get their acts together. They had great jobs and money saved. They just couldn't find a landlord willing to take a chance on them. It seemed like they just continued getting hit with bad news and bad luck. The latest rejection from a potential landlord was the last straw for the wife. She decided that she wanted to end the marriage. (As if that would change anything for the better!) She had handled the first hits to the best of her ability, but with the third one—she just wanted out. Thankfully they are working it out!

In another example, the God Chick of Proverbs 31 was prepared for winter (v. 21). This passage might mean a literal winter (it *is* really tough to prepare for winter here in Los Angeles . . . hmmmm, which bathing suit should I wear? The blue or the black one? ☺). But it is definitely speaking of dark times. She, this incredible woman—you—is prepared for when storms might come. The third punch will not knock her out!

In my storm, on the ship, I have learned patience, because I have discovered that the journey *is* the destination. How I do life is very important. And the truth is, if I do life His way, then the destination will be incredible—far beyond what I could imagine or think! So let's get through our storm. Let's do what we can to endure and escape it. And along the way, let's watch for the glorious shore and people God has prepared for us!

Thanks for taking the time to read my book . . . but more importantly, thanks for being committed to making it through the storms. We are counting on you!

Tholly

p.s. for some study notes, keep on reading . . .

STUDY GUIDE
FOR
STORM RIDERS

Chapter One

1. What storms are you currently riding out?

2. Describe your feelings as you are in this storm.

3. Are you feeling guilty? (Stop that!)

4. What support mechanisms have you put in place to help you through the storms?

5. What Scriptures are you using to brace your mind, so that the truth is more real than the facts?

6. King Solomon wrote "Two are better than one" (Eccl. 4:9). What friend are you holding on to as you ride out this storm? And, because there are others who need you, what friend are you helping through her storm?

Chapter Two

1. Because having hope is crucial to surviving storms, what good can you find in the midst of your tempest? (It may not be easy to see it, but try! Remember, God did not cause your storm, but He will see you safely through it.)

2. How are you choosing to find joy in the midst of your situation?

3. With whom are you sharing joy?

4. In the past, how have you (like Ernest Shackleton) endured something that you really believed was impossible?

5. Smile at three people today . . . no matter what you might feel like!

6. Tell two people something great about your life.

CHAPTER THREE

1. Just for fun: on the last trip you took, did you pack anything you didn't use?

2. What hurts—related to friends, family, finances, school—are you carrying around now?

3. Whom do you need to forgive?

4. What are you afraid of (other than snakes!)? How does that fear affect you today?

5. If you are going to defeat insecurity, you must answer these questions (or at least start thinking about them!): *Why am I important to what God is doing on the earth? How am I making a difference?*

Chapter Four

1. What is the best movie you have seen recently? (Just a little light-thinking in the midst of all of this work you are doing!!)

2. What are three priorities in your life?

3. How much of your time are you putting toward these priorities?

4. What distracts you from your priorities?

5. If today was your last day on Earth, what would you do?

6. How have you gotten sidetracked from a goal you set?

7. If loving is a biblical priority, how can you demonstrate it today?

8. If having a clear conscience is a biblical priority, what might you need to confess?

9. Can you think of a time recently when what you believe (your faith) and what you did (action) did not fall in line with each other?

CHAPTER FIVE

1. To keep ourselves on course in a storm, we have to drop anchors. One of them is *purpose*. What do you think one part of your purpose might be?

2. Knowing who you are is essential in getting through storms. What are some Scriptures that describe how God sees you?

3. What three things are you really good at?

4. How do you want to be remembered?

5. Are you living your life in a way that will cause you to be remembered that way?

6. Are you attending church, or are you actually planted in the house of God? What is the difference?

7. Who is one of the most courageous people you know? What makes him or her brave in the face of storms?

8. Have you lost sight of the shore? Where should your focus be?

Chapter Six

1. Have you been tempted to just quit in some area of life? Has the storm gotten so bad that giving up seems like the best option?

2. How can you keep yourself going?

3. Whom would your decision affect?

Chapter Seven

1. What are some natural things you can do to help you get through the storm?

2. Are you satisfied with your diet?

3. When is the last time you exercised?

4. Are you sleeping well?

5. Are you effective at work—or has the storm overshadowed your abilities?

6. If you are feeling brave, ask someone in your world if you are handling your emotions well during this storm.

7. If you are married, are you loving your husband in practical ways? Has the storm caused you to look away from your marriage?

Chapter Eight

1. Have you let the storm eclipse God?

2. When was the last time you took a few moments to magnify God? How did you do that?

3. Are you willing to admit that you have put your trust in something or someone other than God to get you through this storm (money, a friend, yourself)?

4. Life can be hard . . . but don't you think it is harder without God?

5. Are you allowing Him to be on the throne, or do you keep trying to take over?

6. Do you trust Him?

7. Can you find yourself in Psalm 107? Does the end bring you any peace?

Chapter Nine

1. Is your storm one you stirred up yourself? Or can you remember going through one that you brought on yourself?

2. Like the prodigal son, have you ever felt as if you were entitled to something (money, respect, material possessions)? Are you willing to admit to any self-indulgent behavior?

3. Have you left some relationships—people to whom God has assigned you?

4. While in a storm of your own making, have you ever attached yourself to someone you shouldn't have?

5. How can you humble yourself in this situation?

6. What does repenting mean? Are you willing to do it?

7. When you picture God, is He angry with you or smiling?

notes

INTRODUCTION

1. Jim Reeve, *God Never Wastes a Hurt* (Lake Mary, Fla.: Creation House, 2000), 8.

CHAPTER 1

1. Stu Weber, "Someone to Lean On," *Focus on the Family Magazine,* June 1996, 20.
2. www.sermoncentral.com/timothypeck.
3. Jack Hayford, How to Live Through a Bad Day (Nashville: Thomas Nelson, 2001), 49, 56–57.

CHAPTER 2

1. www.hiscall@cs.com.
2. Reprinted from, "Everyday Hero Lynn Eib: Advocate for Cancer Patients," *Today's Christian Woman* magazine, (July/August 2003), published by Christianity Today International, Carol Stream, Illinois.

3. Walter Anderson, *The Confidence Course* (Harper Perennial, 1997), 157–158.

4. Margot Morrell and Stephanie Capparell, *Shackleton's Way* (London: Nicholas Brealy Publishing, 2001), front flap.

5. Ibid., 13, 82.

CHAPTER 5

1. Robert Schuller, *Tough Times Never Last but Tough People Do* (New York: Bantam, 1984), 150.

2. Stephen Covey, *First Things First* (Free Press, 1996).

3. The Declaration of Independence, 4 July 1776.

4. Rick Warren, *Purpose-Driven Life* (Grand Rapids: Zondervan, 2002), 21.

5. Bobbie Houston, *Heaven Is in This House* (Maximised Leadership, 2002), 26–27.

6. *Today in the Word,* Moody Bible Institute, January 1992, 8.

CHAPTER 6

1. www.Encarta.msn.com

2. www.nyhistory.com/harriettubman

3. www.lkwdpl.org/wohio

4. Jack Canfield and Mark Victor Hansen, *Chicken Soup for the Soul II* (Deerfield Beach, Fla.: Health Communications, 1993), 253.

5. Ibid., 254.

6. Ibid., 253.

7. Brian Zahnd.
8. Ibid.

CHAPTER 7

1. Liz Brody, "Here's to Your Health!" *O, The Oprah Magazine*, April 2003, 130.

CHAPTER 8

1. www.sermoncentral.com/jeremyhouck.
2. Strongs 1453.
3. Mark 4:39 (AMP)
4. Lisa Beamer, *Let's Roll* (Wheaton, Ill.: Tyndale House Publishing, 2002), 69.

CHAPTER 9

1. © Reuben Morgan/Hillsong Publishing (adm in the US & Canada by Integrity's Hosanna! Music) ASCAP c/o Integrity Media, Inc., 1000 Cody Road, Mobile, AL 36695.
2. Reeve, *God Never Wastes a Hurt*, 28.
3. Ibid., 29.
4. Ken Blanchard and Don Shula, *Everyone's a Coach* (Zondervan, 1995).

about the author

Holly Wagner is a popular speaker at conferences around the world, from Los Angeles to Australia, New Zealand, Canada, Scotland, and Wales. She always makes an impact on her audiences, and is known for her challenging, personable, and humorous style of addressing real-life issues. While dealing with situations that are important to us all, she gives powerful and tremendously impacting direction in the areas of building friendships, enhancing marriages, and developing character.

Crowned Miss Texas National Teenager at the age of eighteen, Holly went on to attend Duke University and Southern Methodist University. She then moved to Los Angeles working as an actress in TV, film, and modeling.

Her first book, *dumb things he does/dumb things she does*, published by Thomas Nelson Publishers, offers a humorous yet challenging approach to overcoming relationship obstacles and is garnering national and international attention. *she loves me/she loves me not*, published by Harper Collins, focuses on the relationships between women and offers insight on "Friendship Dos" and

"Friendship Don'ts." Her most recent book, *God Chicks,* is both a challenge and a motivation to women to passionately live out the life they were designed to. Holly has appeared on television's Fox Family Channel, The 700 Club, 100 Huntley Street, On Main Street, Good Morning Sydney, the Australian Beauty and the Beast, and Good Morning Australia, speaking on effective relationships.

Her husband, Philip, is the Senior Pastor of The Oasis Christian Center, in Los Angeles, and together they lead this unique multiracial church that reaches the entertainers of Hollywood, families, and the business leaders in the community. Holly is one of the main teachers in the church and leads a dynamic women's ministry, encouraging women to be who God called them to be.

Holly loves all the parts of her life! She loves being Philip's wife and working on her marriage. She has a great time with her two children, Jordan and Paris, and is often seen cheering for their baseball and basketball teams!

For recreation, she enjoys spending time with her family and friends. She likes to exercise, having earned a black belt in karate, and goes scuba diving with her husband in some of the most beautiful spots in the world!

To contact Holly, please reach her through:
The Oasis Christian Center
5700 Wilshire Blvd. #480
Los Angeles, CA 90036
(323) 937-5433 x 114
www.godchicks.com and www.oasisla.org

acknowledgments

Although my name is on the cover as author, I don't believe any book . . . and certainly not any of mine! . . . is really the work of one person. For twenty years, I have been in the house of God listening and being taught by wonderful men and women of God. Over the years I have listened to countless numbers of teaching tapes, read thousands of books, had conversations with hundreds of people, and spent hours and hours getting to know my God. It is through all of these influences that these words have been penned. I have certainly tried to give credit where credit is due . . . so if I missed you . . . sorry!

I love my church, The Oasis Christian Center. Together we have been on a journey. I owe much of who I am to the incredible people of The Oasis.

And Philip . . . so much of you is in me and in this book. Thank you for the words and the stories. I am stronger and better because of your love and belief in me, and I consider it an honor to be weathering the storms of life with you. I will love you forever!

GOD CHICKS

Holly Wagner believes it is no accident that you and I are alive and on the earth at this time in history…what an awesome privilege it is. Granted, terror is alive and real on the planet, but so are we and the purposes for which we have been placed here.

The King of heaven is waiting for women to take their places on the earth …we have a job to do. Proverbs 31:8-9 says it like this—we are to open our mouths for those who can't speak for themselves; open our mouths for those who are left defenseless; we are to judge righteously and administer justice. How can we do this if we are not confidently living our lives as God's girls on the earth?

In *God Chicks,* Holly encourages women to embrace their God-given roles, such as the Warrior Chick, the Friend Chick, and the Just b.u. Chick. "We are invaluable," says Holly, "and more women need to see themselves this way. We do not have to strive or force our way…we just have to confidently walk as we were created—daughters of a King."

ISBN: 0-7852-6448-5

How to Stop Doing the Things that Drive Women Crazy

How to Stop Doing the Things that Drive Men Crazy

dumb things he does

dumb things she does

HOLLY WAGNER

Love & Marriage/Relationships

THOMAS NELSON PUBLISHERS
Nashville
A Division of Thomas Nelson, Inc.
For other life-enriching books, visit us at:
www.thomasnelson.com

An expert at making potentially complex issues easy to understand, Holly Wagner cuts to the chase and tells both men and women to "wise up"! Her playful, yet challenging, words encourage couples to appreciate their differences and make the most of them.

The dumb things men do—like failing to lead their families, avoiding growing up, and forgetting to keep courting their wives—are covered in the first third of the book. The reversed back third of the book features the dumb things women do, including disliking themselves, failing to demonstrate respect for their partners, and trying to "fix" men. The neutral center section presents the dumb things both sexes do, such as fighting in an unfair way, being unforgiving, and failing to understand the healthy differences between men and women.

ISBN: 0-7852-6520-1